The Netherlands: Revolt and
Independence, 1550–1650

ST. MARY'S COLLEGE OF EDUCATION

'e

Access to A-Level History

General Editor: Keith Randell

The Netherlands: Revolt and Independence, 1550–1650

Martyn Rady

Edward Arnold

© Martyn Rady 1987

First published in Great Britain 1987
by Edward Arnold (Publishers) Ltd
41 Bedford Square
London WC1B 3DQ

Second Impression 1988

Edward Arnold (Australia) Pty Ltd
80 Waverley Road
Caulfield East
Victoria 3145
Australia

British Library Cataloguing in Publication Data
Rady, Martyn
    The Netherlands: revolt and independence,
    1550-1650. - (Access to A-level history)
    1. Netherlands - History - Wars of
    Independence, 1556-1648
    I. Title   II. Series
    949.2'03   DJ156

    ISBN 0-7131-7629-6

The cover illustration shows the market-place at Anvers painted at
the beginning of the seventeenth century, artist unknown.

Text set in Linotron Plantin
by Northern Phototypesetting Co, Bolton
Printed and bound in Great Britain
by J. W. Arrowsmith Ltd, Bristol

Contents

vi   Contents

Preface

To the teacher

The *Access to A-Level History* series has been planned with the A-Level student specifically in mind. The text of each volume has been made sufficiently expansive to allow the reader to complete a section without needing to re-read paragraphs in order to 'unpack' condensed narrative or to 'tease out' obscure meanings. The amount of factual detail is suitable for the requirements of A-Level, and care has been taken to ensure that all the 'facts' included have been explained or placed in context so as to allow proper understanding. Differing interpretations of events are discussed as appropriate and extracts from sources are woven into the main text. This is essential if A-Level students are to be encouraged to argue a case, bringing in suitable evidence to substantiate their points. The hope is that the text will be sufficiently interesting to increase student motivation towards reading history books, and sufficiently stimulating to encourage students to think analytically about what they have learnt.

It is also intended that the series will offer direct assistance to students in preparing to answer both essay and source-based questions. It is expected that the help with source questions will be particularly welcomed. The sections providing guidance to the student which appear at the end of each chapter could be used either as a basis for class discussion or by students when working on their own. Direct help is also given with note making and realistic suggestions are made for further reading.

To the student

Many of you will find that this suggested procedure will enable you to derive the most benefit from each book:

1 Read the whole chapter as fast as you can, and preferably in one sitting.
2 Study the flow diagram at the end of the chapter, ensuring that you understand the general pattern of events covered.
3 Study the 'Answering essay questions on . . .' section at the end of the chapter, consciously identifying the major issues involved.
4 Read the 'Making notes on . . .' section at the end of the chapter, and decide on the pattern of notes you will make.
5 Read the chapter a second time, stopping at each * or chapter sub-heading to make notes on what you have just read.
6 Attempt the 'source-based questions on . . .' section at the end of the chapter.

When you have finished the book decide whether you need to do further reading on the topic. This will be important if you are seriously aspiring to a high grade at A-Level. The 'Further Reading' section at the end of the book will help you decide what to choose.

I wish you well with your A-level studies. I hope they are both enjoyable and successful. If you can think of any ways in which this book could be more useful to students please write to me with your suggestions.

Keith Randell

A Note on Terminology

The sixteenth-century Netherlands extended over the area of the modern-day Duchy of Luxembourg, of the Kingdoms of the Netherlands and of Belgium and, of a part of north-east France (see map on page 4). The Netherlands included at that time two main linguistic groups, Dutch speakers and French speakers (also called Walloons). In the text which follows, 'Netherlands' should be understood in its sixteenth-century sense. 'Dutch' refers only to Dutch speakers or, as an adjective, to that part of the Netherlands which, consisting almost entirely of Dutch speakers, formed after 1579 the separate state of the United Provinces.

CHAPTER 1

Background

1 Historical Origins of the Netherlands

On 19 September 1356 the 14-year-old son of the King of France stood resolutely by his father's side as the flower of French chivalry was cut down before his eyes by English troops at the Battle of Poitiers. For his bravery the boy earned the title of 'the Bold' and it is as 'Philip the Bold' that he is remembered. As a reward from his father Philip received in 1361 the Duchy of Burgundy in eastern France.

Philip the Bold did not become King of France when his father died, for the crown was inherited by his eldest brother. Instead Philip added to the lands he had been given. Besides Burgundy, he acquired by war and marriage Franche Comté (the County of Burgundy), Flanders and Artois. By the time of his death in 1404 Philip's possessions reached from the Swiss border to what is now Belgium. Philip's successors continued the policy of territorial expansion. Over the first half of the fifteenth century the lands belonging to the Duchy of Burgundy doubled in extent to include Holland, Zealand, Hainaut, Mechlin, Limburg and Luxembourg. By the reign of Charles the Rash (1467–77), Philip the Bold's great-grandson, the Burgundian properties lay in an almost unbroken chain along the eastern boundary of France, with a heavy concentration in the Low Countries.

True to his nickname, Charles the Rash's imprudence led to his downfall. Frightened by Charles's aggressive policies, the enemies of Burgundian expansion joined together. Charles was defeated and killed by the Swiss at the Battle of Nancy (1477) and the French King, Louis XI, then invaded the Duchy of Burgundy. Louis would have captured even more of the dead Duke's lands had not Charles's heir, his daughter Mary, hastily married a protector, the Austrian Archduke (later Emperor) Maximilian of Habsburg.

The character of the Burgundian state completely changed in 1477. Firstly, the ruling house ceased being French and became instead Austrian and Habsburg. Secondly, with the Duchy of Burgundy now lost, the main bulk of the state lay in the Low Countries, extending in a roughly triangular fashion from Luxembourg to Flanders and to Holland. After 1477 we can therefore talk of a distinct political and territorial unit known as 'the Habsburg Netherlands'.

The Habsburg Netherlands was passed down from the Emperor Maximilian and his wife Mary of Burgundy to their son, Philip the Handsome, who ruled between 1493 and 1506. Philip married a Spanish princess, Juana of Castile, and became Philip I of Spain. The son of his marriage to Juana was Charles of Ghent, who on his father's death in 1506 became ruler of the Netherlands. In 1516 he was crowned Charles I

The Netherlands in the sixteenth century

of Spain and, three years later, was elected Charles V of the Holy Roman Empire.

Charles V revived the expansionist policies of his predecessors, the Dukes of Burgundy. In 1521 he took Tournai from the French and over the following years occupied Friesland, Utrecht, Overijssel and Gelderland (see map on page 4). It is probable that Charles planned to extend the Habsburg provinces of the Netherlands southwards by taking Lorraine, and it is certain that he wanted to recapture the Duchy of Burgundy lost to France in 1477. But Charles's many obligations as King of Spain and Holy Roman Emperor prevented him fulfilling these ambitions.

Until the middle of the sixteenth century, the 17 provinces of the Netherlands (Holland, Zealand, Brabant, Utrecht, Overijssel, Flanders, Walloon Flanders, Artois, Luxembourg, Hainaut, Mechlin, Namur, Groningen, Friesland, Gelderland, Limburg and Tournai), comprised territories technically belonging either to the Holy Roman Empire or to the French Crown. Charles changed this. In 1526, 1529 and 1544, after having soundly defeated him in battle, Charles made the King of France renounce his rights to the 'French' provinces and recognise them as fully independent Habsburg territories. Then, in 1548, Charles won the agreement of the Imperial Diet (the law-making body for the Holy Roman Empire) to all the 'German' provinces of the Netherlands becoming independent of the Empire. The next year, in the 'Pragmatic Sanction' of 1549, Charles had the laws of succession in all 17 provinces changed to ensure that the ruler of each would always be the same person. Charles V thus achieved full sovereignty and statehood for the Netherlands and, as he thought, the assurance that a Habsburg would continue to rule over all parts of the new creation.

Throughout Charles's reign the Netherlands remained the least of his problems. The Emperor's principal concerns were his wars with France and the struggle against the Protestant princes in Germany. Charles was therefore content to leave the Netherlands under the care of a regent, the first of whom was his aunt Margaret of Austria and the second, after 1531, his sister Mary of Hungary. Although resentment of Charles's repeated demands for taxes occasionally spilled over into isolated acts of rebellion, the Netherlands remained free of any large-scale uprising. Yet, little more than a decade after Charles's abdication in 1555 the Habsburg Netherlands was in revolt and had become the most urgent problem facing Charles's son, Philip. During Philip's reign, the state built up by Charles split in half and for 80 years – from 1566 to 1648 – he and his successors were engaged in a bloody and losing fight there against the forces of sedition and rebellion.

2 The Structure of Government

During Charles's reign all 17 provinces recognised the same ruler and, when he was absent from the country, the authority of the regent appointed by him. The parliaments or estates of the provinces sent delegates to attend a 'general parliament' or States-General which negotiated directly with the regent and ruler. In every province there was a governor or *stadholder* appointed by the ruler to see that his orders were correctly carried out. A 'national' government functioned in Brussels with powers extending to all parts of the country.

Despite these central institutions, the Netherlands remained only superficially united. Throughout Charles's reign the provinces and towns of the Netherlands exercised powers which gave them a large degree of local autonomy. The markedly decentralised structure of government is most apparent in the list of titles held by the ruler, in the organisation of the States-General, and in the variety of laws and privileges belonging to the individual parts of the Habsburg Netherlands.

The ruler of the Netherlands did not enjoy any single title like 'King' or 'Grand Duke'. Instead Charles appeared in official documents as 'Duke of Brabant, Limburg, Luxembourg and Gelderland, Count of Flanders, Artois, Hainaut, Holland, Zealand and Namur, Lord of Friesland and Mechlin *etc.*' Behind this formula lay the assumption that the Netherlands did not form a single political unit but was instead a confederation of separate parts. In the States-General the idea of confederation was taken a step further. The 'general parliament' of the Netherlands was attended by deputies from each of the separate provinces. But before the deputies could give their assent to any measure, they had to consult with the estates of the various provinces which they represented. And in many provinces the members of the estates had themselves to consult the towns and communities which had appointed them. Decision making was therefore slow, for in both the States-General and the provincial estates a cumbersome process of reporting back had to be followed. Since, in addition, the States-General and the provincial estates had to record a unanimous vote before any decision could be reached, one town could easily obstruct the passage of business in the States-General.

The ruler had to promise at the start of his reign to maintain all local rights and procedures. The laws of the Habsburg Netherlands were complex and differed from province to province and even within provinces. Altogether there were about 700 different legal codes in the Netherlands. Also, every town and community had its own special privileges, while many customs and rights survived which had never been written down. In framing his decrees the ruler had to be careful not to infringe local laws and liberties for otherwise his orders would be deemed invalid.

Linguistic disunity added to the divisions within the Habsburg Netherlands. In the northern and central portions of the Netherlands Dutch was spoken, while in the south a French dialect called Walloon predominated. The Dutch language itself had two main dialects, West

Dutch and Oosters, and in the far north there was another variant called Fries. Although the eventual division of the Netherlands into two separate states did not at all follow linguistic frontiers, the diversity of languages within such a relatively small geographical area may have hindered the development of a specifically 'Netherlandish' national identity and made the goal of political unification all the harder to achieve.

3 Society and Economy

Throughout the Middle Ages the most powerful social group in the Netherlands had been the aristocracy and their influence persisted into the sixteenth century. Particularly in the south, great tracts of land lay in the hands of just a few families. Most of these families had a history which stretched back to the Middle Ages and had a truly international character. The Egmont and Hornes families were, for instance, related by marriage to the great French house of Montmorency. The House of Orange-Nassau, wealthiest of all the aristocratic families of the Netherlands, was of German origin and owned estates in the Empire, Italy and France: the principality of Orange was in fact in southern France. Although many of the aristocracy, or grandees as they are often called, held lands in the northern provinces of the Netherlands, the countryside there was dominated by the lesser nobility, some of which had a lifestyle indistinguishable from that of the better-off peasantry. Many of these noblemen were clients of the grandees and were obliged by feudal loyalties to do their lords' bidding.

During the sixteenth century the economic position of both aristocracy and lesser nobility started to suffer. A sudden spiral of inflation pushed up the cost of living, while the income available from landownership remained static because rents were fixed. Invariably the nobles failed to adjust their expenditure to meet their reduced circumstances. They preferred to borrow money rather than lower their standard of living.

*While the aristocracy and lesser nobility sank into penury, the towns of the Netherlands prospered. The Netherlands probably had the greatest concentration of towns in the whole of Europe. By 1550 19 of its cities had a population of more than 10 000; England by contrast had only three. Most of the towns were situated in the western, coastal provinces and of these the largest by far was the town of Antwerp, on the River Scheldt, with about 80 000 inhabitants (see map on page 4). The population of the Netherlands at this time was about three million.

Antwerp was primarily a trading centre. It dealt in Spanish and Portuguese cargoes of spices, salt and wool, in German metals, English cloth and luxury items from Italy. As far as native exports were concerned, Antwerp was the principal distributor of the locally-produced
See Preface for explanation of * symbol.

and finished textiles. Altogether three-quarters of the trade of the Netherlands passed through the town making it the most important commercial centre in north-west Europe.

Antwerp's dependence on foreign trade made it vulnerable. In the 1540s the Portuguese withdrew from the town to develop their own port at Lisbon. The decay of the German metals industry, which was unable to compete with the bullion of the New World, deprived Antwerp of its commerce with central Europe. Business with England was disrupted by currency changes in the 1560s and then by a commercial rivalry which led to an embargo on trade. In 1569 English merchants left Antwerp altogether for Hamburg. By this time the deteriorating political condition in the Netherlands had set Antwerp on its course of rapid decline.

Even before the onset of the slump in Antwerp's trade, the towns of Holland in the north had begun their meteoric rise to prosperity. About two-thirds of the province of Holland lay under water. The construction of dykes and the draining of polders (low-lying land reclaimed from the sea) was insufficient to make the cultivation of land possible on a large scale. Holland's population had therefore to look abroad for cereals and for basic foodstuffs. During the sixteenth century the merchants of Amsterdam, Rotterdam and Haarlem were active in trade with the ports along the Baltic shore where they purchased grain both for their own province and for the rest of the Netherlands. Gradually they extended their business to other commodities: wine, textiles, metals and salt. In addition, the maritime population of Holland and of neighbouring Zealand engaged in fishing cod and herring in the North Sea which were exported after salting for foreign consumption. The commercial rise of Holland and of Amsterdam, which was fast becoming the province's foremost town, is reflected in population figures. Censuses from the early sixteenth century reveal a population rise in the province of 30 per cent in just two decades, while between 1514 and 1550 the number of Amsterdam's inhabitants trebled to reach 30 000.

* At the top of the social hierarchy in the towns were the patricians (sometimes misleadingly called 'regents'), who were mainly the better-off merchants and financiers. The patricians dominated the municipal councils which ran the towns, and prevented all but the very wealthy from joining their ranks. In this way the patricians preserved political and economic supremacy in their communities. Lower down the social scale were the guildsmen and shopkeepers. At the bottom were those craftsmen who were excluded from the guilds, and the mass of labourers and casual workers. The last group were in times of slump likely to find themselves unemployed and close to starvation. On such occasions the poor were liable to join with the guildsmen in uprisings against the ruling patricians. Without exception these protests were put down.

By the mid-sixteenth century the Netherlands was entering a period of social and economic change. The aristocracy and lesser nobility were in decline; the towns were increasing in size and importance, particularly in

Holland where they would soon outstrip Antwerp. These developments were to exercise a strong influence on the course of the subsequent rebellion. The Revolt would be started by the aristocracy and nobility, anxious to maintain their political leadership in the face of their declining economic power, but the Revolt would be sustained by the towns of the north. Their commercial strength would provide the economic resources for bringing the Revolt to a successful conclusion. And, because the patricians were never ousted from their position of dominance in the towns, their achievement would be the establishment of a middle-class republic.

4 Religion

Throughout the first half of the sixteenth century the government of Charles and of his regents, Margaret of Austria and Mary of Hungary, proved accommodating and flexible. The aristocracy were regularly consulted and their advice was taken in all great matters. In the central government in Brussels, particularly in the Council of State, the grandees were given a leading role. In the provinces they were entrusted with *stadholderates* (provincial governorships) and with military commands. The States-General was summoned regularly – more or less annually – and Charles heeded its recommendations, scrapping plans for reform if too many objections were raised. Even in the matter of taxation – Charles's huge empire required large injections of cash to keep it running – the ruler listened. The persistent complaint of the States-General that Charles was demanding too much money forced the Emperor during the 1540s to endeavour to borrow more from the merchants and to tax them less. Despite this, the level of taxation in the Netherlands grew sevenfold during Charles's reign. The fact that the States-General agreed to this increase is a comment on Charles's ability to win the confidence and trust of this body.

   * It was in the matter of religion that Charles encountered his greatest difficulties and where his preferred method of 'government by consent' faltered. Charles was a devout Catholic who felt that both the office of Emperor and the example of his predecessors obliged him to defend the faith whatever the cost. Early on in his reign, Protestantism started to spread into the Netherlands from Germany and began to take root there among all classes – among the nobility, peasantry and the townsfolk. Charles reacted vigorously, promising that the heretics would receive no mercy. In 1520 the first Protestant books were burnt and the first decree was issued against the new faith. Penalties were severe. During Charles's reign the death sentence was made mandatory not only for those who attended Protestant services or who professed heretical beliefs but also for those found guilty of just possessing a Protestant book or translation of the Bible. Altogether about 2000 heretics were burnt during the period of Charles's rule.

It may well have been, as one critic of the burnings pointed out, that such severe treatment of heretics made martyrs of them and encouraged others to deviate from the established faith. By the close of Charles's reign, though, it would seem that persecution was working. Protestantism had not established the solid core of popular support in the Netherlands which made it such a formidable force in Germany. Neither did the movement enjoy the patronage of the powerful, nor did it have an effective underground organisation. Except in the larger towns, like Antwerp, and in the more remote areas of the countryside, where detection was difficult, heresy had been largely eliminated in the Netherlands.

Charles's achievement in restraining heresy was made at the cost of alienating the upholders of law and order in the localities. Firstly, the heresy laws infringed many established rights. The Inquisition of the Netherlands was the principal agency enforcing the religious laws. It claimed the right to arrest and try heretics in all parts of the country, even though local laws and privileges laid down that an offender could only be judged by the magistrates of the community in which he lived. Secondly, magistrates were reluctant to prosecute offenders knowing the awful penalty they faced. During the second half of Charles's reign the heresy decrees regularly contained a list of the punishments which might fall on those tardy local officials who did not carry out the ruler's wishes. Thus according to one decree issued by Charles in 1540:

1 Justices and officials who have seized the aforementioned heretics
   or Anabaptists shall not conceal them along with their accomplices
   and abettors or punish them less severely than they deserve with
   the excuse that the penalties are too severe or harsh and only
5 imposed to frighten delinquents, as we have found has often happened in the past, under pain of forfeiting their rank and functions,
   being declared unfit for office and otherwise punished as we think
   suitable.

Despite such threats, some law officers in the towns and provinces continued to turn a blind eye to protestant religious practices. In fact, owing to the laxity of officials it proved easier during the 1550s to be a heretic in some parts of the Netherlands than in the England of Mary Tudor (1553–58). Thus one English exile wrote, explaining her flight to Antwerp:

1 The reason why we did think ourselves safer in Antwerp than in
   England was not for any more liberty of the gospel given there, but
   because there were not parish churches but only a cathedral:
   wherein though the popish service was used, yet it could not be
5 easily known who came to church and who not. But there was a
   chapel for the English merchants and thereunto all of them were

compellable to go upon solemn feast days to wait upon the governor. And the night before that day my good husband would lie
mourning in his bed and could not sleep for grief to think that he
10 was on the morrow to go with the governor to that idolatrous
service. But the governor, though he was a papist, yet he was no
persecutor nor cruel papist, for he was contented to bear with my
husband, so far as he might without being seen to do it, and would
say to him that though he did bark yet he did not bite . . .
15   And thus I continued in Antwerp till the death of Queen Mary,
which was not a little joyful to me to hear of; for during the time of
her tyrannous reign I had often prayed earnestly to God to take her
or me forth of the world. In all which time I never was present at
any of the popish masses, or any other of their idolatrous services.

It appears, therefore, that while the persecution of heresy was on the
whole effective, it revealed differences between the Brussels government
and officers of law enforcement like the governor here. During the reign
of Charles's successor, the problem of applying the heresy laws assumed
additional significance under the impact of Calvinism.

5 The New Ruler

In 1555 Charles abdicated. He was succeeded as Holy Roman Emperor
by his brother Ferdinand. Charles's possessions in Spain, Italy, the New
World and the Netherlands were inherited by his son Philip II. The
Netherlands thus became the property of the King of Spain. During the
first years of Philip's reign the Netherlands saw a new wave of heresy.
The ideas of John Calvin, originating in Switzerland, spread and won
converts. Calvinism, with its missionary organisation and easily understood theological structure, proved attractive to a wide social spectrum.
Although Calvinism's appeal was greater in the towns, nobles and
peasants were also drawn into membership of reformed churches.
  It would seem unlikely that Calvinists made up in the early 1560s any
more than a few per cent of the population, but Philip was alarmed at the
growth of this new heresy. As a devout Catholic he was committed to
maintaining his faith as the exclusive religion. His response to Calvinism
was to step up persecution by ordering magistrates to proceed 'with the
utmost rigour' against the heretics. Nonetheless many local officials
continued to conceal offenders, and secret Calvinist congregations
gathered. In those regions where persecution was most intense, Calvinists fled abroad, to England, France and Germany. There they awaited
events and sent pamphlets, Bibles and trained Calvinist clergy to their
fellow believers in the Netherlands.
  * In his severe treatment of heresy Philip was following the example of
his father. He did not inaugurate the policy of repression. However, in
his approach to government Philip broke away from Charles's principle of

compromise. In the four years between 1555 and 1559, when he ruled the Netherlands from Brussels, Philip demonstrated a clear disregard for established rights and procedures which was bound to cause resentment.

First of all, Philip made few concessions to aristocratic sensitivities. Unlike Charles, he spoke neither Dutch nor French and never made any attempt to do so. Nor did Philip adapt to the ways and temperament of the country. As the group most commonly used to dealing personally with the ruler, the grandees were particularly offended by Philip's uncompromisingly Spanish manner. The contrast between Philip and his father was stark and it provoked comment from a Venetian observer:

1 Philip takes excessive pleasure in being revered, and he maintains
   with everyone, no matter who he may be, a greater haughtiness
   than his father, a fact which his subjects, except for the Spaniards,
   are not happy about. And indeed they have good reason, being
5 used to his father, who knows extremely well how to adjust himself
   by various ways to all kinds of people. It seems as if nature has
   made the Emperor capable of satisfying the Flemings and Burgun-
   dians by his habits of familiarity and informality, the Italians by his
   talents and wisdom, the Spaniards by his reputation and severity.
10 His subjects, who now see the son behaving otherwise, feel not a
   little displeasure at this change.

However, the growing rift between ruler and grandees had its origin in rather more than just a severe and haughty manner. Throughout his reign Philip's distrusting and suspicious nature led him to place confidence in only a small band of counsellors and officials. These depended directly on him for their salaries and promotion, and he therefore felt able to rely on them. But he had no such way of manipulating the allegiance of the grandees of the Netherlands. Their lands, status and prestige were inherited; they were not the gifts of the ruler. Because Philip could not control the grandees by patronage he did not trust them and did not involve them in the business of government.

Philip additionally upset relations with the States-General. This was largely because he failed to understand the principle of 'give-and-take' which governed all successful dealings with this body. Instead of bargaining behind the scenes as Charles and his regents had done, Philip tried to make the States-General bow to his will. When in 1557 the deputies of the town of Brussels impeded the passage of business in the States-General, jeopardising the grant of a subsidy, Philip threatened to have Brussels' privileges suspended. Although this extreme measure was not put into effect, it made the States-General distrustful of him. The States-General, encouraged by the grandees, began to insist that it be given a greater control of the revenues it voted. It was no longer prepared to hand over money to the ruler unconditionally.

Philip's main reason for staying in the Netherlands after his accession in 1555 was to coordinate the war with France. In 1559 peace was made with the French King and Philip prepared to return to Spain. Certainly in the first years of his rule Philip had made mistakes in the Netherlands and had embittered relations with both the aristocracy and the States-General. However, there was nothing as yet to suggest that the country would depart from the peaceful condition it had enjoyed during Charles's reign. Therefore Philip's advisers all agreed that their master's overriding concern must be the Mediterranean, which was in danger of becoming a 'Turkish lake'. The lands by the North Sea could, it was argued, spare their ruler.

Making Notes on 'Background'

Although the span of this chapter covers the two centuries from 1356 to 1559 its content relates mostly to the reign of Charles V and the early years of Philip II of Spain's rule. The following headings and questions will help you make notes:

1.   Historical origins of the Netherlands. Compose a date-chart covering the years 1356, 1361, 1477, 1506, 1521, 1526/29/44, 1548, 1549.
Explain in what ways Charles V 'achieved full sovereignty and statehood for the Netherlands'.
2.   The structure of government.
In what ways was the Netherlands more a confederation of separate states than a single state?
3.   Society and economy
3.1. Aristocracy and lesser nobility
3.2. Antwerp and the towns of Holland
3.3. The urban hierarchy
What social tensions were present in the Netherlands which might lead to disaffection later on?
4.   Religion
4.1. 'Government by consent'
4.2. Protestantism
What dangers did religious persecution bring to the ruler?
5.   The new ruler
5.1. Calvinism
5.2. Philip II
How did Philip's government of the Netherlands differ from his father's?

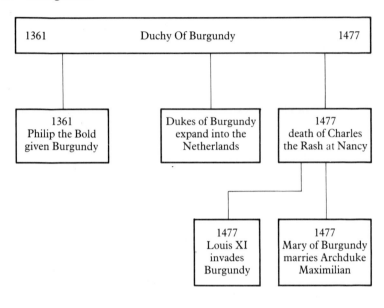

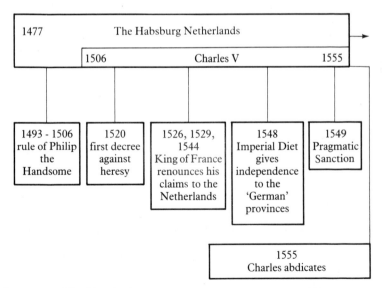

Summary – The historical origins of the Netherlands, 1361–1555

Answering essay questions on 'the Netherlands during the early sixteenth century'.

It is not an exaggeration to say that at least one question on Charles V occurs every year in the examination papers of each A-level Board. Sometimes a question will involve one aspect of Charles's reign: his government of Spain or his dealings with the German Protestants, for instance. Occasionally though, the question will be more general:

'How successful was Charles V?'

'To what extent were the problems faced by Charles V of his own making?'

In questions like these some treatment of the Netherlands will be required, but you will need to devote the bulk of your essay to Charles's relations with France and with the German princes, to his ordering of Spain and to general matters such as his concept of empire and his financial limitations.

Only very infrequently do specific questions occur on the Netherlands during the first half of the century:

'Why was the Netherlands a greater problem for Philip II than for Charles V?'

Plan this essay by writing six sentences beginning 'Because'. The result will provide the skeleton for your answer. You should consider not only how Philip's method of rule was bound to cause him more difficulties than his father, but also how social, economic and religious changes in the Netherlands introduced additional problems for Philip.

Source-based questions on 'Background'

1 Religion
Read carefully the extract from a heresy decree issued in 1540 (page 10) and the account written by an English exile in Antwerp during the 1550s (page 10–11). Answer the following questions:
a)   What evidence is there in the heresy decree to suggest that magistrates were evading their obligation to arrest heretics?
b)   Why according to the English exile did the ecclesiastical organisation of Antwerp make it safer for a heretic to live there?
c)   Explain why 'solemn feast days' might pose a special problem for Protestant refugees in Antwerp?

d) What do you imagine to be the role of the governor as mentioned in the exile's account (lines 7–15)? To what extent does the governor's behaviour support the accusation made about the conduct of officials in the heresy decree of 1540?

CHAPTER 2

The Revolt 1566–76

1 The First Conflict

Before departing for Spain in 1559 Philip appointed his half-sister, the Duchess Margaret of Parma, as regent of the Netherlands. By choosing a close relative as his regent Philip continued the policy of his father, whose own regents had been his aunt and sister respectively. Since, in contrast to her predecessors, Margaret's experience of government was slender, Philip feared that she would soon become a puppet of the aristocracy. For this reason, before he left the Netherlands he set up a *consulta* or 'inner council'. The council consisted of three loyal servants of the crown and their principal task was to advise the regent and ensure that she kept to the instructions sent to her by Philip. Head of the council was Antoine Perrenot de Granvelle, who was a native of Franche Comté. Granvelle was a shrewd and experienced politician but from Philip's point of view Granvelle's most important qualification was his slavish devotion to his royal master.

During the period between 1555 and 1559, when Philip had ruled the Netherlands from Brussels, the grandees had been largely excluded from influence in the court. With Philip and his accompanying counsellors now gone, the grandees hoped to be readmitted to the centre of political power and decision-making in the Netherlands. Most of all, the grandees expected that the Council of State, on which they sat, would once again act as the main source of advice for the regent, just as it had during Charles's reign.

The appointment of an inner council and the influence exerted by this body over the regent disappointed the grandees. Accordingly, a group of them, led by the Counts Egmont and Hornes and by Prince William of Orange, the *stadholder* of Holland, Zealand and Utrecht, began a vigorous campaign against the council and against Granvelle in particular. Soon after Granvelle's appointment as a cardinal in 1561, the three grandees and their supporters donned jesters' caps in mockery of the cardinal's own red cap, and in speeches and letters made plain their ambition to have Granvelle dismissed.

The grandees were confident of winning their campaign against Granvelle. Firstly, they were convinced that Philip was so harassed in the Mediterranean, where he was at war with the Turks, that he would be unable to pay much attention to events in the Netherlands. Secondly, the grandees believed that they had in their campaign against Granvelle powerful friends in the Spanish court who were as anxious as they to curb the cardinal's influence. In addition, Egmont, Hornes and Orange reckoned themselves virtually immune to reprisals should their plotting miscarry. Each belonged to an ancient and distinguished family which

William of Orange aged 22, by Antonio Moro

had served both Spain and the Netherlands well in the past. Moreover, Orange in 1561 married into the ruling house of Electoral Saxony. He optimistically reckoned that, should his scheming backfire, his bride's German relatives would support him with an army.

★ In fact the grandees chose their ground well and Granvelle fell bloodlessly. In 1561 Philip ordered a thorough reform of the ecclesiastical organisation of the Netherlands. Following a plan originally devised by his father, he proposed the creation in the Netherlands of 14 new bishoprics which would entirely displace those foreign sees under whose jurisdiction the ecclesiastical affairs of the country were currently placed. The new prelates would require an income. So he planned that they would also be appointed abbots of nearby monastic houses and would take over their revenues. To make them perform their spiritual duties properly, he stipulated that the new bishops should have been educated in theology and that each should be equipped with inquisitors to check up on the moral and religious orthodoxy of their flocks.

Philip's scheme threatened, unintentionally, nearly all the influential forces in the Netherlands. As abbots traditionally sat in the provincial parliaments, representatives in these assemblies expected that the new abbot-bishops would form among themselves a pro-Spanish lobby. For their part, the nobles traditionally regarded a career in the church as suitable for younger sons without lands of their own. The new arrangement promised to close down this avenue of employment as the children of nobles normally thought that theological training was beneath them. Finally, the appointment of inquisitors was seen as the preliminary to a new wave of religious persecution. With Calvinism spreading in the country, this could only mean more arrests and burnings, the prospect of which was repellant to many.

Granvelle had played little part in devising the bishoprics plan. Nevertheless, as the scheme envisaged him being promoted primate of the Netherlands, he became the focus of discontent. At the grandees' instigation, the provincial parliament of Brabant pressed for Granvelle's dismissal and coupled its request with a refusal to collect taxes. The nobility joined in the chorus. In the towns pamphlets and flysheets sang the same tune. One particularly scurrilous piece depicted Granvelle as a hen hatching a brood of bishops. Above his head was drawn the Devil, speaking the words, 'This is my beloved son'. Eventually the regent could no longer withstand the clamour of her subjects. In the summer of 1563 she gave in and petitioned Philip for Granvelle's removal. Philip took her advice. The next year Granvelle was withdrawn from the Netherlands, eventually to rejoin the court in Madrid, and the bishoprics plan was drastically modified to quell objections.

★ With Granvelle gone, the power of the inner council was broken and the grandees were restored as the regent's principal advisers. They were now determined to consolidate their triumph and use their newly returned influence to moderate the heresy laws. Their reasons for embracing the cause of greater religious freedom were threefold. Firstly the grandees saw in the recent example of France evidence that the ruthless persecution of heresy could lead directly to civil war and they feared that if Philip persisted with his religious policies the same tragedy might befall the Netherlands. Secondly, the mechanism of persecution as practised by the inquisition suggested a strong disregard for established laws and procedures. It was in the aristocracy's interest to uphold traditional freedoms in general, for among these might be counted their own right to be heard by the ruler and regent. Finally, the grandees, although they were Catholics, were generally not zealous in their faith, and they saw no reason why differences of belief should be treated so harshly. As Orange forcefully put it in one meeting of the Council of State, 'However strongly I am myself a Catholic, I cannot approve of princes attempting to rule the conscience of their subjects'. In December 1564, the Council with Margaret's approval sent Egmont to Spain to request Philip's permission for the heresy laws in the Netherlands to be relaxed. Egmont's mission was a failure. Philip rejected the request.

* Although the grandees had been thwarted in their bid to have the heresy laws changed, they had given hope to others who, unlike them, were prepared to add the threat of violence to petitioning. During the winter of 1565–66 an alliance of lesser noblemen known as the 'Compromise' was organised. Its initiators were mainly Calvinist sympathisers but the purpose of the Compromise – the relaxation of the heresy laws – attracted the support of about 400 nobles, most of whom were Catholics. In April 1566 the confederates, as the supporters of the 'Compromise' were known, rode into Brussels with pistols thrust conspicuously into their belts. There, they presented a petition to the Regent demanding an end to persecution. The confederates' petition was composed politely, with repeated protestations of loyalty to both King and Regent. However, in their manner and speeches the leaders of the Compromise made it plain that should Margaret refuse their demands they would resort to arms.

Although one of Margaret's advisers was so unimpressed with the confederates that he christened them 'Beggars', the Regent understood well the significance of their organisation. A sizeable section of the nobility, upon which the preservation of law and order in the provinces depended, was threatening rebellion. Furthermore, the cause of the Beggars had become a popular one, as the shouts on street corners of *Vivent les Gueux* (Long live the Beggars) and the sale of decorative begging bowls amply demonstrated.

With the grandees of the Council generally sympathetic to the confederates, Margaret had no choice except to give in. The day after receiving the confederates' petition, she ordered inquisitors and magistrates to proceed from now on 'discreetly and modestly' in investigating heresy. Because her authority did not technically extend to making such an order, Margaret sent envoys to Madrid asking Philip to approve her measures. In presenting Margaret's case, they stressed the growing unease in the Netherlands and told how only the lenient treatment of heresy could prevent disorder. Despite the urgency of the envoys' message, it was not until four months later that Philip's response, which allowed a few minor concessions, was delivered to Brussels. By this time its modest contents had been rendered out-of-date by the progress of events.

   * The Calvinist movement in the Netherlands was fed during the early 1560s by Huguenot refugees who, on fleeing the French religious wars, found that local magistrates in the Netherlands were often ready to overlook Protestant religious practices. As a result of their immigration there were by 1566 about 300 places in the Netherlands where Calvinist congregations regularly met. When news came in April 1566 that the heresy laws were no longer to be applied rigorously, local Calvinist preachers for the first time forsook secrecy and those leaders and congregations still in exile abroad hastened back to their homeland. As one contemporary put it, 'All the vermin of exiles and fugitives for religion, as well as those who had kept in concealment, began now to lift up their heads and thrust forth their horns.' Throughout the long summer of 1566 huge outdoor services were held outside the major towns. In most places the congregations were allowed to meet without any interference by the local forces of law and order.

   Many of those attending the open-air services came only out of curiosity or fashion. However, the crowds gave confidence to those who addressed them and, so emboldened, the preachers embarked on a dangerous course. During August and September, mobs were urged on by inflammatory sermons to invade churches throughout the Netherlands. Catholic centres of worship were ransacked and ceremonial items were torn out as an affront to the 'pure worship' of Calvinism. Hundreds of churches were desecrated. The 'Iconoclast Fury' (an iconoclast is one who destroys images; statues and paintings were the special targets of the mobs), while led by a hardcore of extremists, yet enjoyed considerable support, as this account of events in West Flanders suggests:

1 Some few of the vilest of the mob, to whom several thieves and prostitutes had joined themselves, were those that began the dance being egged on by nobody knows whom. Their arms were staves, hatchets, hammers, ladders, ropes, and other tools more proper to
5 demolish than to fight with; some few were provided with guns and swords. At first they attacked the crosses and images that had been erected by the great roads of the country; next, those in the villages; and, lastly, those in the towns and cities. All the chapels, churches and convents which they found shut, they forced open, breaking,
10 tearing and destroying all the images, pictures, shrines and other consecrated things they met with: nay, some did not scruple to lay their hands upon libraries, books, writings, monuments, and even the dead bodies in churches and churchyards. Swift as lightning,

Iconoclasts at work

the evil diffused itself, insomuch that in the space of three days
15 more than four hundred churches were plundered. In some places
the magistrates themselves pulled down the images, to prevent the
mob from doing the same.

Such a description makes the Iconoclast Fury seem little more than
vandalism. Actually, iconoclasm was the first act in the establishment of
a new church-system in the Netherlands. By throwing out the parapher-
nalia of Catholic worship from the churches, the Calvinists were claiming
these as their own. With the buildings cleansed of items insulting to God,
they could be used for the reformed faith.

The Iconoclast Fury was so widespread and unexpected as to divide
the grandees from the confederates. Up to this point the aims of the two
groups had been broadly similar, although the approach of the confederates was more heavy-handed. Disturbed by the collapse of authority,
Orange, Egmont and Hornes now rallied to Margaret and undertook to
pacify the country by negotiation. Meanwhile, the confederates took
advantage of the chaos to petition the Regent for more concessions. In
desperation, she agreed in August 1566 to complete freedom for Protestant worship in the more troubled regions. Privately Margaret notified
Philip that she could no longer control events. She exaggeratedly
reported the triumph of heresy and that 200 000 of her subjects were
armed and mutinous. Suitably alarmed at Margaret's reports, Philip
decided to gather a Spanish army ready to impose order by force on the
Netherlands.

News of the King's preparations lent Margaret a new resolve. She
angrily dismissed talk of more concessions and, indeed, began to go back
on her previous undertakings. In December 1566 she imposed garrisons
of loyal troops on the main centres of unrest, the 'bad towns' of Flanders.
When the inhabitants of these towns refused entry to their garrisons,
they were cut down. In defence of the beleaguered Calvinists, the
confederates mustered their own forces, which were in turn defeated in a
series of small engagements. By the late spring of 1567 order had been
returned to the Netherlands and Calvinism had been driven underground once more. The grandees played a loyal role in the restoration of
the Regent's authority, providing both troops and military expertise.

2 Alva

Philip's reaction to the 'troubles' in the Netherlands can only be understood in the context of his own deeply felt commitment to the Catholic
faith. At the height of the disorders of 1566, he wrote to Pope Pius V,

1 Before suffering the slightest damage to religion and the service of
God, I would rather lose all my estates, and a hundred lives if I had
them, because I do not propose, nor do I desire, to be the ruler of

heretics. If it can be, I will try to settle the matter of religion
5 without taking up arms, because I fear that to do so would lead to
total ruin. But if I cannot settle matters as I wish without force . . .
neither the danger nor the destruction of all I possess can deter me
from this end.

Philip was resolutely determined to prevent heresy taking root in the
Netherlands. Margaret's desperate appeals for help and her exaggerated
account of conditions confirmed Philip's belief that the heretics would be
content with nothing less than the destruction of the Catholic faith. With
news of the Iconoclast Fury and Margaret's own admission that her
policy of conciliation had failed, Philip was left with only one option –
force. Support for a policy of no compromise came from the court in
Madrid, the Spanish capital, where a 'war party' led by the Duke of Alva
had recently emerged. In the first years of Philip's reign, the dominant
faction in the Madrid court had been led by the Duke of Eboli. Eboli and
his supporters had pressed the King to make concessions in the Spanish
territories abroad and generally favoured the creation of a more decentralised empire. Partly it was the influence of the Eboli faction in Madrid
which had earlier convinced the grandees that their assault on Granvelle
would succeed, for Granvelle and Eboli were bitter rivals. However, the
calamities which followed Granvelle's fall undermined Eboli's standing.
In place of him, the Duke of Alva, who leaned towards a more rigidly
structured empire, became Philip's main adviser. By September 1566,
under Alva's influence, Philip was ready to support Margaret with
troops. Preparations were begun for the despatch of an army northwards
from Italy to the Netherlands and Alva was appointed commander. In
June 1567 the Spanish troops began their passage across the Alps.
    By this time, of course, the rebellion had been crushed. But Philip was
not convinced that Margaret's letters advising him to call off the expedi-
tion really could be trusted. Had not she said the previous summer that
200 000 Netherlanders were on the verge of mutiny? Furthermore, the
reports Philip received from his spies in the Netherlands suggested that
Margaret was so indebted to the grandees for their part in suppressing
the rising that she would not be able to restrain their ambition to gain
complete control of the country for themselves.
    With news of Alva's mission and imminent arrival, those who had
played a leading part in the recent rising did their best to flee. They were
joined by Orange. Although he had helped Margaret restore order, his
earlier plotting had endeared him neither to Spain nor to the regent.
Warned that Philip regarded him as a dangerous meddler who merited
punishment and that Margaret would not protect him, Orange left for
Germany in April 1567.
    Four months later Alva's army entered the Netherlands. Its comman-
der was a grizzled veteran, now 60 years of age, who had served the
King of Spain in the German, Italian and French wars. Alva's present

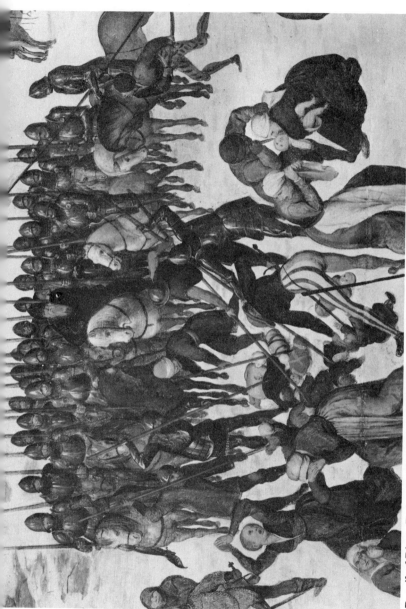

Detail of Pieter Bruegel's 'Massacre of the Innocents'. Some scholars have suggested that the horseman in black is the Duke of Alva

orders were to restore peace and eliminate heresy in the Netherlands. On the basis of these instructions, Alva considered himself not a subordinate of the Regent, but rather as immediately responsible to Philip. So Alva felt able to ignore Margaret in matters of religion and public order. Not surprisingly the two fell out. When, without consulting her, Alva arrested Egmont and Hornes, later to execute them, Margaret resigned. Philip appointed Alva as her replacement, giving him the title of Governor-General.

   * The main instrument by which Alva sought to fulfil his orders was the Council of Troubles or, as it was nicknamed, the Council of Blood. The Council of Troubles was primarily a judicial body set up to investigate and punish heresy. More than anything else, it has blackened Alva's reputation among historians who have seen the Council as a cruel instrument of Spanish repression. The Council was, though, staffed principally by Netherlanders. In the provinces it was supported by tribunals which were entirely administered by native officials. The Council's enquiries were largely initiated by denunciations. The view, therefore, that the Council of Troubles was a uniquely Spanish institution bent on subjugating a cowed people is debatable.

   Between 1567 and 1576 the Council found guilty just under 9000 persons of whom about a thousand were executed, the rest having fled. The Council also saw to the confiscation of goods belonging to condemned heretics and refugees. Their possessions, if in the form of property, were leased out by the new government yielding a considerable income. Such treatment of confiscated wealth was held to be contrary to most local law. Thus the accusation spread that the main purpose of the Council was steadily to destroy liberties in the same way as it was grimly taking lives.

   The Council of Troubles is the glass through which Alva has often been viewed. Similarly many historians have frowned on the portrait of Alva in Pieter Bruegel's picture, the *Massacre of the Innocents*, where the Duke is seen as a sort of Herod presiding over the slaughter of children in an unhappy Dutch village. In fact, as Professor William Maltby has recently shown (see Further Reading, page 113). Alva's government was on the whole not unjust and certainly not without achievement. Alva saw to the completion of the bishoprics plan earlier devised by Philip, and ensured that the new prelates were sensible and serious about their work. He investigated and improved the quality of the universities, increasing professorial salaries to attract talented scholars. In 1570 he caused the reforming 'Ordinance of the Penal Law' to be issued which standardised procedure in criminal cases and ensured protection in law for the innocent. Even the Dutch historian, Pieter Geyl, otherwise a bitter critic of Alva, concedes the Ordinance to be 'in many respects, an excellent piece of work'.

   Despite these achievements, Alva's régime in the Netherlands became almost universally detested: as much by the majority of loyal

Catholics as by the minority of persecuted Calvinists. The main explanations for Alva's unpopularity must be sought firstly in the propaganda
of his enemies and, secondly, in Alva's demand for new taxes.

★ The exiles who fled the Netherlands after the rising of 1566–67 set
up sanctuaries in England, Germany and France. From these places they
unleashed on their homeland a torrent of flysheets and pamphlets con-
demning Alva and his troops. They presented the aim of Philip and Alva
to be the total destruction of the Netherlands and its conversion into a
slave state of the Spanish empire. The activities of the Council of
Troubles were wildly exaggerated so that, 'All trees on the roads, all
gallows on the places of execution are everywhere full of innocent people.
All market-places are blazing with the fires in which simple folk are burnt
alive; the canals are filled with dead corpses.' Selecting the occupying
troops as a vulnerable target for criticism (since like all soldiers of the
time they were guilty of excesses), pamphlets told of their relentless
raping of women and of their contaminating the land with syphilis. A
particularly powerful myth depicted Spanish soldiers ripping unborn
babies from their mothers' wombs and throwing them against walls.
Later, the Spaniards were charged with cannibalism. To the modern
reader such accusations appear crude and obviously false. In the Netherlands of the sixteenth century, though, rumour was the main source of
news, while unsophisticated and frightened minds were prepared to
believe much of what they heard.

★ Alva had with him in the Netherlands 10 000 Spanish troops, about
4000 local recruits and a varying but sometimes colossal number of
foreign mercenaries. In 1572 his entire army stood at little less than
70 000 men. Such a huge organisation incurred equally large costs.
However, Philip's own finances were in poor straits and he was unable to
find funds in Spain for Alva's army. Alva was therefore told to extract the
money he needed from the local population.

Accordingly in March 1569 Alva summoned the States-General to vote
new taxes. Although the deputies proved generally compliant, they
refused outright the tax known as the 'Tenth Penny': a ten-per-cent tax
on all sales and transactions. Alva had pinned most of his hopes on having
this source of revenue accepted. Because the Tenth Penny was designed
as a permanent tax, he would not have to haggle yearly with the States-
General for its renewal. The States-General, though, foresaw in the
Tenth Penny the ruin of trade and a means of bypassing its right to
control taxation. It therefore permitted only a levy which was to be paid
over two years and raised in the traditional manner. Alva agreed and for
the next two years his government was reasonably solvent. When the tax
voted in 1569 expired, Alva began talks again about the Tenth Penny.
Now he was told that the States-General would agree to no such measure;
nor would it renew the levy authorised in 1569. Alva decided to impose
the Tenth Penny tax without the permission of the States-General. In
March 1572 troops were moved into shops and warehouses in Brussels to

see to the forcible collection of the tax. Retailers and business owners responded by closing down their workplaces and by bringing the economic life of the great cities to a halt.

3 1572

In April 1567 William of Orange had fled the Netherlands for his German estates. He had not yet decided to become a rebel but judged it best to await events from a position of safety. In 1567 Alva was still an unknown quantity and to test the ground Orange sent him a letter congratulating him on his appointment and asking whether he could be of service to the new regime. In response he was condemned in his absence by the Council of Troubles and his estates in the Netherlands were confiscated. His former colleagues, Egmont and Hornes, were beheaded.

The punishments meted out by the Council of Troubles left the Prince of Orange with no choice but to assume the role of rebel. Furthermore, with Egmont and Hornes gone and the chief confederates either dead or dispersed, Orange saw himself as the leader of opposition to Alva. However, he realised that he could not challenge Alva's rule without a struggle. So in 1568 the Prince invaded the Netherlands with the help of a mercenary army gathered in Germany. The campaign was a complete failure. Orange's troops were rapidly defeated; not one town rose up against Alva in Orange's name.

Over the next four years, Orange did his best to restore his fortunes and increase the number of his allies. In 1567 he had converted to Lutheranism, an act which it is hard to believe was motivated by anything other than political considerations. As a Protestant he now called on the aid of his co-religionists in exile. Looking to France, he established close links with the Huguenots, even fighting alongside them in their wars against the French Catholics. By his deeds Orange won over the Huguenot leader, Admiral Coligny, who by 1571 was the dominant voice in the court of Charles IX of France. Most importantly, Orange carefully presented himself while in exile as a 'national leader' and 'father of his country', whose overwhelming concern was the overthrow of a tyrannical régime. In pamphlets and letters he listed the crimes of Alva's government and promised to restore the lost liberties of his countrymen.

 ⋆ By the early months of 1572 Orange had ready a second invasion plan. The Netherlands would be invaded from Germany by two armies. Meanwhile, a mixed force of exiles and Huguenots would attack from France. They would later be supported by a French army led by Admiral Coligny. From the sea a fleet fitted out by Orange and presently at anchor off the French coast would attack Holland and Zealand. The fleet would be helped by privateers who sailed under Orange's flag in the North Sea and were commonly known as the 'Sea Beggars'. Orange, though, did not estimate the Sea Beggars highly and they were not vital to his plans. As it happened, it was the Sea Beggars who proved the most decisive military factor in the events of 1572. Thanks to them, Orange and the rebels acquired a permanent foothold in the Netherlands from which it proved impossible to dislodge them.

* The Sea Beggars were a motley mixture of pirates, exiled noblemen and Calvinist seafarers who had been previously drawn to Orange's side to provide maritime support in the failed invasion of 1568. After Orange's defeat they survived mainly by piracy. They harrassed the coast of the Netherlands and attacked both Spanish and neutral shipping, selling captured vessels in England for cash. But their activities were so damaging to trade that in March 1572 Queen Elizabeth expelled them from their refuges on the English coast. With nowhere else to go, they sailed to Holland and on 1 April seized the unguarded port of Brill. Encouraged by the ease of their victory, they took Flushing three weeks later. By May the Beggars had carried their occupation into the heart of Holland and Zealand.

It was once thought that the Sea Beggars owed their success to the popular support their cause attracted in the northern provinces of the Netherlands. In fact, in the light of recent research, it now seems that the Beggars' rapid conquest of Holland and Zealand owed far more to the actions of small groups of town officials desperate to preserve their position as local leaders.

By 1572 the government in Brussels was calling on all town councils in the Netherlands to collect the Tenth Penny tax without delay or face fines and confiscations instead. Resistance to the tax was strong in Holland. In April 1572 the estates of the province noted 'unrest everywhere among the populace amounting almost to a general revolt and confusion'. As the local magistrates were the officials who had to collect the Tenth Penny, they began to fear revolutions in the towns. In Gouda pikemen were employed to guard the townhall against attack by the citizens. As it was, economic conditions were already quite appalling. The tradesmen's revolt against the Tenth Penny, combined with Sea Beggar activity on the coast, had brought commerce to a complete standstill. Unemployment and starvation were the consequence. Moreover, as news of the Beggars' successes spread, the fear followed that Spanish troops would shortly be marched north against the invaders and billeted on the luckless townsfolk.

Isolated by their appointment as collectors of the Tenth Penny and frightened as to what lengths hunger and fear might drive the commonfolk, the rulers of the towns were in no position to resist the arriving bands of Beggars. In town after town they opted for the Beggars' cause. Thereby they were at least assured of some measure of protection, of staying in office, and of not having to collect the new tax. These advantages outweighed their fears of future Spanish reprisals.

On any other occasion Alva could have subdued the small band of rebels in one swift campaign. But in May 1572, just one month after the seizure of Brill, Orange's assault on the Netherlands began. All Alva's forces had to be diverted to its repulse. The invaders met with instant success. In contrast to 1568, they were aided by local risings: a comment in itself on the degree to which Alva's régime had by now thoroughly alienated the population. By July, a good part of the north-east and of the province of Hainaut lay in the hands of Orange's supporters. The next month, the prince invaded Brabant.

However, Alva had regained the initiative by the autumn. A sudden and bloody change of policy in the French court (heralded by the St Batholomew's Day Massacre) robbed Orange of Coligny's aid. With superior forces and no longer fearing a French thrust into the Netherlands, Alva was able to push the rebels northwards. On the way, he horribly sacked Mechlin and Zutphen. By November 1572, the Prince of Orange was once more in flight. This time, though, he did not seek safety in Germany but chose instead as his refuge the still unvanquished provinces of Holland and Zealand.

4 Holland and Zealand

The area of safety to which Orange fled in 1572 did not even include all of Holland and Zealand. Holland's chief town, Amsterdam, remained an enemy outpost while the greater part of Zealand remained loyal to Spain. Holland and Zealand were mostly waterlogged territories with only a sparse population.Seemingly, they had neither the resources nor the manpower to defy Spain for long. Yet defy they did and they provided in the end the springboard for the conquest of the northern half of the Netherlands.

The resistance of Holland and Zealand was more than just a military one. For within these provinces was brought about a constitutional revolution which decisively tilted the political balance away from monarchy towards parliamentary rule. In this way, the struggle of Holland and Zealand against Spain became as much a conflict between two fundamentally opposed systems of government as a simple 'war of liberation'.

Ever since 1555, the year of Philip's accession, the power of the ruler and of his representative had been expanded in the Netherlands at the expense of local privileges and traditional rights. Alva's rule had taken this development a step further. Under Orange's guidance this trend was reversed in the rebel provinces. Orange had previously promised to return their lost freedoms to the people of the Netherlands. In Holland and Zealand he soon fulfilled his commitments. In July 1572 Orange communicated his wish and promise to the estates of Holland that,

1   They shall discuss and ordain the best and most suitable means of restoring and reestablishing in their old form and full vigour all the old privileges, rights and usages of the towns, which may have been suppressed and taken away by Alva's tyranny . . . His Highness

5   has no other purpose than to restore under the lawful and worthy
reign of the King of Spain the power, the authority and reputation
of the estates to their former condition in accordance with the
privileges and rights which the King has sworn to maintain. And
without the estates, His Highness shall not endeavour to do or
10   command anything that concerns the provinces or that may be
harmful to them . . . His Highness binds himself to undertake or
command nothing without the advice or consent of the estates or at
least the majority of them, and without consulting these estates and
countries if and when they desire this. To this end, the estates and
15   the delegates of the towns shall swear to His Highness to be faithful
to him for ever and not to desert him, but to assist him in every
possible way.

Orange's undertakings may of course be interpreted as an expression
of belief in parliamentary government. More obviously, though, Orange
was in this communication attempting to enlist support. In 1572 his
power was still very limited. The rebellion of Holland and Zealand was
largely the work of the Sea Beggars who, although they fought in
Orange's name, were intensely independent. Moreover, to continue
fighting, Orange needed cash. The towns alone possessed reserves of
wealth and only they, through the provincial estates, could impose taxes.
Again, after Orange's defeat and flight in 1572 his natural authority was
gravely weakened. To maintain his influence, Orange had to concede a
partnership in government to the estates.
    The arrangement prospered. In 1572 Orange was confirmed by the
estates as *stadholder* (governor) of Holland, Zealand and Utrecht. These
offices had originally been given to Orange by Philip; with the estates'
permission Orange now used these titles as a way of justifying his
authority in the rebel provinces. Orange was also made responsible for
the defence of Holland and Zealand: a task he performed successfully.
When in 1575 the two provinces accepted a formal union, Orange was
made head of the combined government. In turn, the estates appointed
committees to advise the prince on all matters of government and war.
Their deputies sat in Orange's councils of state and finance. The decrees
of the *stadholder* were issued in the name of 'His Excellency and the
Estates'. A parliamentary régime was thus installed in Holland and
Zealand, with powers shared jointly by Orange and the estates. Earlier
on, Orange had talked of a constitutional restoration. By 1576 he had
engineered a constitutional revolution.
    * The constitutional revolution was accompanied by what has since
been called 'the revolutionary reformation'. Originally both Orange and
the estates had intended a full measure of religious toleration. In July
1572 the estates of Holland had promised freedom of worship 'to Reformed and Roman Catholic, in public or in private, in church or in chapel'.
However, this commitment soon gave way. In the summer of 1572 fresh

outbreaks of iconoclasm erupted in the towns occupied by the Sea Beggars. Churches and monasteries were ransacked; priests were murdered. Early in 1573 Orange had the most violent Beggar leaders arrested for their excesses. Although this act served Orange well politically, for it removed a potential source of opposition, it did not resolve the religious conflict. Returning exiles fanned the unrest and by the spring the exercise of the Catholic religion had to be banned in the interest of public order. In town after town, churches were seized and taken over by Calvinist congregations.

Although it is doubtful that Orange ever became a Calvinist in the matter of his own beliefs, he did in April 1573 become a member of the Calvinist church. Nevertheless, the triumph of Calvinism as 'the established religion' in Holland and Zealand was not necessarily approved of by the majority of the population there. Numerically the Calvinists remained a very small group and certainly well under ten per cent. In many places the proportion was much less. Furthermore, the Calvinist churches were ill organised. In theory they possessed a complicated structure of organisation made up of consistories, presbyteries and synods; in practice they lacked even the pastors to see to the needs of their few congregations.

* The successful resistance of Holland and Zealand to Spain cannot, therefore, be explained by the inspiration of Calvinism. Instead, the failure of Alva and of his successor to restore royal rule in Holland and Zealand must largely be put down to three quite different factors: the geography of the Netherlands, the mistaken strategy adopted by the Spanish and the financial weakness of Spain.

The rebel provinces were later described by an English traveller as 'The great Bog of Europe. There is not such another marsh in the world. They are an universal quagmire: epitomiz'd *A green cheese in pickle, the ingredients of a black pudding.*' Holland was crossed by dykes while Zealand consisted entirely of islands. Great rivers – the Waal, Maas and Ijssel – cut through the provinces providing a natural barrier which forced invaders to make long detours. Marshes and lakes added to the problem of movement. In this terrain the rebels resorted to a form of guerrilla warfare which wore out their opponents. They also made good use of the water. In 1573 and 1574, they broke the dykes to relieve the sieges of Alkmaar and Leiden. On the flooded polders the rebels' shallow-drafted boats moved unheeded.

By concentrating their attacks on the towns of the region, the Spaniards hoped to drive the rebels away from their main source of wealth and manpower. The war thus became an exhausting succession of sieges. The towns of Holland and Zealand were in many cases well fortified and defended with the most up-to-date protection: the bastion, a type of rampart not easily destroyed by artillery-fire. Furthermore, the inhabitants of these places resisted the Spaniards vigorously, with a determination motivated by fear. Alva, contrary to the accepted conventions of warfare, was apt to have terrible revenge on the towns once they had fallen, so the conviction was sown among the defenders that the only hope of survival lay in resistance.

The continued war in the Netherlands was a constant drain on Spanish resources. In 1572 all attempts by Alva to collect the Tenth Penny were abandoned and the main cost of the war fell on Spain. As the conflict deepened, expenditure rose. By 1572–73, Spain was subsidising Alva to the tune of 3½ million florins a year; by 1574 this figure had doubled. These were the very years when Spain was shouldering the fight against the Turks in the Mediterranean without allies. Philip was unable to continue paying for two wars simultaneously and the Spanish treasury moved to the verge of bankruptcy.

* By this time Alva's failure was only too obvious. In November 1573 he was replaced, later returning to Spain in disgrace. His successor was the former governor of Lombardy, Luis de Requesens. For the first year of his appointment Requesens continued Alva's policy of war. In April 1574 he scored a notable victory against the rebels, defeating their army in a rare full-scale engagement at Mook. But still unpaid, the victors of Mook mutinied; those garrisoning the Spanish outposts in Holland joined them. Although the mutineers were brought back under army discipline, their action convinced Requesens that the time for negotiation had arrived.

Requesens met the leaders of the rebels at Breda in March 1575. He had the King's permission to make concessions, for, by now, Philip knew that the Spanish finances could not support the war much longer. Requesens therefore offered to withdraw all Spanish troops from the Netherlands. However, the King's conscience would not extend to allowing heresy to flourish in the wake of a withdrawal. All Requesens could offer in the matter of religion was that the Protestants be allowed six months in which to leave the Netherlands unhindered. Since Orange and the estates of Holland and Zealand would not accept this condition, Requesens had no choice but to break off the talks and renew the fighting. Hereafter, events followed swiftly. In September 1575, Philip finally declared the Spanish state bankrupt and the flow of cash to the Netherlands immediately stopped. In the March of the next year Requesens died, leaving behind no successor. Finally, in the summer of 1576, having received no pay for two years, the entire Spanish army mutined and began plundering the provinces of Brabant and Flanders.

5 The Pacification of Ghent

In the war against Holland and Zealand, the fifteen 'obedient' provinces were only the reluctant allies of Spain. Although Philip, Alva and Requesens might explain the war as one justly waged against rebels and heretics, in the troubled towns and countryside of the Netherlands the conflict was perceived as serving only the interests of Spain. By degrees this discontent turned into a bitterness which was directed against the occupying forces. The Spaniards' destructive campaigning, their persistent demands for taxes, the insults of their troops, and the government's seeming disregard for the ancient rights and liberties of the country fed a dislike of Spain which grew dangerously. As one Spanish official in Brussels reported, 'Believe me, the people abhor our nation more than they abhor the devil.'

Resentment of Spanish policy and methods was voiced by the provincial estates which protested loudly against the 'tyrannical behaviour' of the Spanish troops and against the 'general mismanagement of the country'. However, for fear of arrest the deputies were at this stage unwilling to take their resistance further. Instead they looked to the grandees who were traditionally the leaders of opposition to unpopular policies.

* Throughout the decade 1566–76 the aristocracy of the Netherlands kept loyal to Philip II and to the Catholic faith. Alone among the grandees Orange took the rebel's part and changed his religion. The grandees, though, while maintaining their allegiance to Spain, resented the centralisation of authority in the hands of the governor-general and their continued exclusion from decision-making. Behind the scenes, therefore, they plotted to restore their influence in public affairs – just as Egmont, Hornes and Orange had done in the early 1560s. Like these, the grandees demanded that the Council of State, on which they still formed the majority despite the inclusion of Spaniards, be made the principal instrument of government.

The grandees' chance came in March 1576. Requesens died without any successor having been named. In Spain Philip dallied, not knowing whom he could trust to take on the task of ruling the Netherlands. As a result of his indecision, political authority in the Netherlands passed to the Council of State which, according to custom, automatically assumed the reins of government when there was a vacancy above.

The grandees' first inclination was to avoid making any change of policy. They were mindful of the fate of Egmont and Hornes and they had no wish to be accused of treason by the King. So the Council ordered the war to be pursued until instructions to the contrary were received from Madrid. However, the mutiny of the Spanish army in the summer of 1576 made any continuation of the war quite impossible. Within a short time not only were the Spanish troops refusing to obey the commands of the Council, but they were also devastating the towns and countryside of the 'obedient provinces'.

* The mutiny of the Spanish army was accompanied by an appalling savagery. In Brabant and Flanders the mutineers collected their arrears in pay by plundering the local population. Even those communities which had remained conspicuously loyal were subjected to violent looting. The worst atrocities occurred in November 1576 when Spanish troops stormed Antwerp. In the sack of this once great city the Spaniards

systematically tortured the inhabitants to make them reveal where they kept their valuables. Even the monasteries and nunneries were forced to give up their treasures. When not chasing gold, the Spaniards hunted down the womenfolk, subjecting them to gang-rape and a humiliating death. In the three-day orgy of the 'Spanish Fury' about 8000 of Antwerp's citizens were slain and nearly a third of the town was burnt down.

Even before the Sack of Antwerp a shock-wave of anti-Spanish revulsion had swept the country. Orange took advantage of this. During the summer and autumn of 1576 his agents visited the leading members of the provincial estates and urged them to join forces with the Prince to expel the marauding Spaniards from the country. Meanwhile, the helpless Council of State was divided over what its future course of action should be. One group, led by the Spanish councillor De Roda, advocated waiting on events until fresh instructions came from Philip. The other, under the guidance of the President of the Council, the Duke of Aerschot, and supported by the majority of the councillors and grandees, recommended urgent measures to put down the mutiny. In particular, Aerschot asked that a meeting of the States-General be called to coordinate a military response to the mutiny. But De Roda's party blocked this, fearing that once called the States-General would present demands which were bound to displease the King. Thus frustrated, Aerschot opened up negotiations of his own with the Prince of Orange and with the leaders of the estates.

* The coup came on 4 September, 1576. Troops gathered by the estates of Brabant entered Brussels and arrested the Council of State, releasing only those councillors who were in Aerschot's favour. Two days later, the estates of Brabant and Hainaut issued a general summons for a meeting of the States-General. In the mean time, Aerschot and his fellow grandees were installed in a reformed Council of State which at once gave its assent to the calling of the States General. In the period before the States-General assembled, units of the armies of Holland and Zealand entered the south to assist in the defence of the southern provinces against the mutineers.

The States-General which met in Ghent during the autumn of 1576 was united in its determination to end the damaging conflict with the north and to eject the rampaging Spanish army from the country. For these purposes, the States-General immediately entered into talks with the estates of Holland and Zealand and with the Prince of Orange. The product of their discussions was the Pacification of Ghent, signed in November 1576. By the terms of this treaty, the rebel and the obedient provinces put aside their previous differences and agreed to combine forces against the mutineers. The States-General thereupon began to recruit and field its own army which engaged in joint manoeuvres with the men of Holland and Zealand. But over the more contentious issues of the future government and religious complexion of the Netherlands, the Pacification was distinctly evasive. It simply said that all discussion of these weighty matters should be deferred to a later meeting of the States-General which would be called after the mutineers had left the country. Until then, the political and religious organisation of the Netherlands would be frozen in its present form, with Calvinism and the authority of the Prince of Orange confined to Holland and Zealand.

The coup of 4 September 1576 and the Pacification of Ghent which followed have been portrayed as the start of the 'third revolt' of the Netherlands: the previous two being the rising of 1566 and the rebellion of Holland and Zealand in 1572. It should be noted, though, that the signatories to the Pacification proclaimed their allegiance to the King of Spain and explained their union against the mutineers as an essentially loyal act designed to rid the Netherlands of these 'enemies of His Majesty'. Of course, the protestations of loyalty made by the representatives of Holland and Zealand seemed unconvincing even then. But the fact that they were expressed indicates that the Pacification was not intended to deepen the estrangement between Philip and his subjects in the Netherlands, but rather to establish the basis on which reconciliation might take place. And indeed, when early in 1577 the new governor-general eventually appointed by Philip, his half-brother Don John of Austria, entered the Netherlands, he was accepted by the States-General. Don John promptly paid off the mutineers, agreed in the 'Perpetual Edict' to uphold the terms of the Pacification and promised that from now on the liberties of the Netherlands would be respected. For a brief period it seemed that the Pacification of Ghent had successfully restored peace and order to the Netherlands under the rule of the King of Spain, and that the Revolt was ended.

Making Notes on 'The Revolt 1566–76'

The following headings and questions should help you:

1.   The First Conflict
1.1.   The grievances of the grandees
1.2.   The bishoprics plan
1.3.   The assault on the heresy laws
1.4.   The 'Compromise' of the confederates
1.5.   The Iconoclast Fury
To what extent were the grandees responsible for the events of 1566–67?
2.   Alva
2.1.   Alva's mission
2.2.   The Council of Troubles
2.3.   Propaganda
2.4.   The Tenth Penny

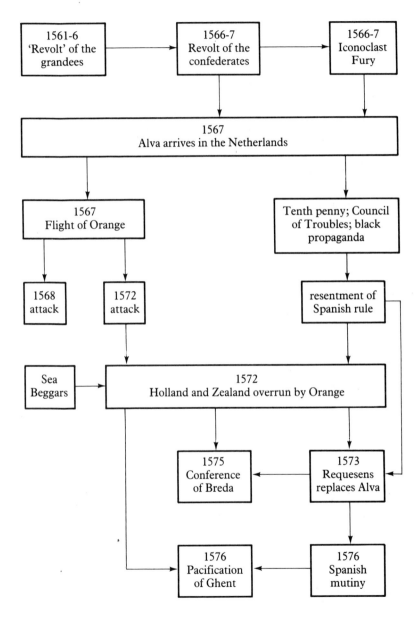

Summary – The Revolt, 1566–76

How did Alva's government of the Netherlands increase opposition to Spanish rule there?
3.   1572
3.1. Orange, 1567–72
3.2. The invasion plan of 1572
3.3. The Sea Beggars
Why did Orange's invasion of 1572 prove more successful than his attack in 1568?
4.   Holland and Zealand
4.1. Orange's partnership with the estates
4.2. The 'Revolutionary Reformation'
4.3. The defence of Holland and Zealand
4.4. Requesens
To which did the successful defence of Holland and Zealand owe more: Dutch strengths or Spanish weaknesses?
5.   The Pacification of Ghent
5.1. Resentment of Spanish rule
5.2. The Grandees
5.3. The Mutiny
5.4. The States-General and the Pacification of Ghent
To what extent did the Pacification of Ghent provide a framework for a lasting peace?

Answering essay questions on the immediate causes and early course of the Revolt 1559–1576

Occasionally A-level questions will ask you to analyse the initial stages of the Revolt, looking in particular at who or what was responsible for its outbreak and at why the rebellion could not be crushed in its infancy:

'Why was there a Revolt in the Netherlands in 1566?'

'Imagine that you are a Spanish official in the Netherlands in the mid-1570s. Write an assessment from your own point-of-view of the origins and character of the Revolt.'

The first of these questions requires substantially more than just an account of what happened in the period 1559–66. Divide your essay into two parts. The first part should be devoted to long-term causes: economic and social tensions; Philip's style of government; the problem of heresy. For information on these factors, look back to your notes on the first chapter of this book. The second part of your essay should analyse the more short-term causes: the actions of the grandees and the part played by the iconoclasts and confederates. In your conclusion, weigh up whether the Revolt of 1566 was the inevitable product of the changes going on at this time in the Netherlands or whether it was caused by political mismanagement on the part of Philip II and Margaret of Parma.

The second question is in a form which you may have already encountered at O-level or GCSE. The main purpose of this type of question is to see whether you can put yourself in the shoes of a person living in the past and correctly identify the attitudes and prejudices of the time. However, what you write should not be vague but will need frequent references to real historical events and characters – otherwise the examiner may think you are 'waffling'. It frequently happens with this type of question that eagerness to expose the prejudices of the past leads to factual inaccuracies. Be careful not to fall into this trap.

Source-based questions on 'The Revolt, 1566–76'

1 The Iconoclast Fury
Read the account of the Iconoclast Fury in West Flanders on pages 21–23 and the text of Philip's letter to Pope Pius on page 23. Look at the picture of iconoclasts at work on page 22. Answer the following questions:
a) What evidence is there in the account of the Iconoclast Fury to suggest that this outbreak of violence was (i) spontaneous, and (ii) organised? Can this apparent contradiction be explained?
b) To what extent does the picture of iconoclasts at work support the written account of the Iconoclast Fury? What differences are apparent?
c) How do you explain the iconoclasts' particular choice of targets?
d) Bearing in mind Philip's comments to the Pope in his letter of 1566, how would you expect him to act on receiving news of the Iconoclast Fury in the Netherlands?

2 The government of Holland
Read the letter sent by William of Orange to the estates of Holland in 1572, which is given on pages 30–31), and look at the picture of Alva reproduced on page 25. Answer the following questions:
a) Explain the terms 'privileges', 'estates', 'countries'.
b) Of what does Orange allege the government of Alva to have been guilty?
c) With reference to his picture, the *Massacre of the Innocents*, do you think Pieter Bruegel would have agreed with Orange's description of Alva's regime? Explain your answer.

d)   What type of government does Orange promise to introduce to
     the province of Holland? What does Orange ask to be given in
     return?

CHAPTER 3

William of Orange

1 Orange's Position in 1576

Early in 1576 Orange appeared a spent force. Certainly, he had established a working relationship as *stadholder* with the estates of Holland and Zealand and had altered his own religious views to fit in with the changing religious balance of power of the north. He had successfully defended the rebel provinces against the armies of Philip II. But there seemed little chance that Orange would break through the line of garrisons which hemmed him in and would carry the standard of rebellion into the 'obedient provinces'. On the occasion of its last major engagement with the Spaniards, at the Battle of Mook (in 1574), Orange's army had been pitifully crushed. Guerrilla actions and a successful war of defence might prevent the Spaniards from taking advantage of their supremacy on the field, but such tactics did not amount to a strategy for final victory.

Orange's plight was recognised abroad. Elizabeth I of England regarded his chances of victory as too slender to justify support, while in Brussels it was said that the Prince had 'run out of breath'. Orange, it would seem, agreed with this verdict. He spoke of being 'abandoned by the world', of 'defending ourselves even to the last man', and of how his eventual defeat would at least cost the Spaniards dear.

Orange's contribution to the coup of 4 September 1576 remains obscure. His agents had over the preceding months been at work among the leaders of the provincial estates, advising them of their need to come to terms with the Prince. The commander of the troops which arrested the Council of State was in close contact with Orange. Aerschot also had established relations with the Prince. But whether it was Orange, Aerschot or some other figure who arranged the coup cannot on the basis of the surviving evidence be determined precisely. All that can be said is that Orange took advantage of the event, moving troops into the south and sending commissioners at once to Ghent to conclude a treaty with the States-General. Even so, Orange's influence remained limited. Aerschot and the new Council of State were reluctant to give him any position of authority in the south since this might diminish their own power. As it turned out, the Council's attitude mattered little, for once the States-General met, the Council of State assumed much less importance. But the States-General was remarkably volatile and not yet ready to accept Orange's leadership. Indeed, ignoring Orange's words of caution, the States-General chose to come to terms with Don John and to sign a truce with him, the Perpetual Edict of 1577, the terms of which Orange strongly opposed. It may well be, as Professor Swart has argued (see Further Reading, page 112), that the Pacification of Ghent benefited

Orange by removing the threat to Holland and Zealand, and by effectively recognising the régime he had constructed there. Nevertheless, in the months immediately following the Pacification, Orange's influence and authority did not increase significantly.

2 The Aims of William of Orange

Throughout the 1560s and 1570s, Orange acted as the leader of the opposition to Spanish rule in the Netherlands. During this time Orange's beliefs and intentions changed as he reacted to new circumstances and became influenced by different ideas. It is important to appreciate this development, for otherwise motives may be read into Orange's early actions which in fact only prompted him much later on in his career.

Although his parents were Protestants, Orange had been brought up by Catholic guardians in the Netherlands. There is no evidence that in his youth Orange was a secret Lutheran. Nor, however, is there much to suggest that he was a serious Catholic. Most likely, Orange was throughout his life a *politique*: one for whom political expediency counted for more than deep thoughts on religious issues. As one contemporary put it, 'Observe his inconsistency in religious matters and you will see that he put the state above religion.' Possibly also, as Geoffrey Parker has argued (see Further Reading, page 112), Orange looked back to the 'glorious anarchy' of the early years of the Reformation when a variety of beliefs were tolerated. Either interpretation, though, will explain why Orange would have found repugnant the spirit of the Counter-Reformation with its zeal for Catholic conformity and for persecution. In his opinion, dogma was insufficiently important to warrant punishment and death for those who deviated from its narrow definitions.

Towards the end of his life Orange explained how in 1559 he learnt of a conspiracy to eliminate heresy in Europe and how this inspired him to consider rebellion:

1   When I was in France I was told by King Henry that the Duke of
    Alva was negotiating about ways to exterminate all suspected
    Protestants in France, in this country [the Netherlands] and
    throughout Christendom. I was moved by pity and compassion for
5   so many worthy persons doomed to slaughter, and for this country
    to which I owed so much into which they planned to introduce the
    Inquisition in a form even worse and more cruel than it was in
    Spain, and I confess that when I saw the nets put out to trap both
    the nobles of the country as well as the common people, and that no
10 escape was possible, since one had to do no more than look askance
    at an image to be sentenced to burn at the stake, I deliberately
    began my endeavour of helping to drive the Spanish vermin from
    the country.

It may well be that the unspoken commitment Orange made in 1559 to rid his country of the Spaniards later earned him the nickname 'The Silent'. Clearly, however, he was not silent for long. Within a few years Orange made clear his opposition to religious persecution in meetings of the Council of State and, following Granvelle's fall, he pressed the Regent to moderate the heresy laws. Eventually, as we have seen, Margaret of Parma did so, the Iconoclast Fury erupted, and in the aftermath of its suppression Orange fled the country.

Orange in exile needed the support of the French Huguenots and after 1572 of the Calvinist leaders in Holland and Zealand. Accordingly he embraced the Protestant faith: Lutheranism in 1567 and Calvinism in 1573. Nevertheless, he did not deviate from his conviction that differences of belief did not merit punishment. At the time of his first invasion of the Netherlands in 1568 he ordered his captains not to molest Catholic communities – 'Let them be overcome', he said 'not by violence but with gentleness'. Later on, Orange instructed the magistrates in Zealand not to persecute Anabaptists nor to demand of them oaths which their religious beliefs made it impossible for them to swear. Even during the 1580s, when the struggle with Spain was at its height, ¡and when Catholicism was in the opinion of many of Orange's supporters indistinguishable from treason, Orange did not depart from his earlier views. As he pointed out in 1581, there were 'among the adherents of the Roman Catholic Church many honest and patriotic men and some of them have done their duties honourably.'

* Orange's consistency in the matter of freedom of conscience, despite his own change of faith, contrasts with his attitude towards the political and constitutional organisation of the Netherlands. During the earliest years of Philip's reign, Orange remained completely loyal and was rewarded in 1559 with the offices of *stadholder* of Holland, Zealand and Utrecht. At this time Orange never expressed any doubt that it was the prerogative of the ruler to govern as he saw fit. He even went so far as to declare that anyone refusing to grant Philip the taxes he needed should be hanged.

Philip's reluctance to give the grandees the share of influence to which they felt they were entitled forced Orange into opposition. Following Philip's departure in 1559 Orange led the attack on Granvelle and broke the power of the inner council, previously set up to advise Margaret of Parma. However, at this stage Orange had no intention of achieving anything other than a restoration of what he believed to be the rights of the grandees and of their instrument, the Council of State. Although in the conflict with Granvelle Orange enlisted the support of the States-General, he made it clear that in his opinion the States-General was an inferior body to the Council. Orange's conservative political outlook at this time is demonstrated by his response to the events of 1566–67. Once the Calvinists and confederates had gone into open rebellion, Orange hastened back to the Regent's side and gave his support to the traditional focus of order and authority in the Netherlands.

Following his flight in April 1567 Orange's political views changed rapidly. In the space of a few months, from being the leader of the aristocratic opposition to Philip II, he became instead the advocate of popular rights and privileges. In an open letter written after his flight he explained his aims as the following:

1 We seek for each and every estate, lord, knight, nobleman, captain, bailiff, sheriff, steward, burgomaster, alderman, tax receiver, guild, trade, civic guard and burgher, and for all the good inhabitants of the Netherlands, freedom and deliverance from the
5 present enslavement by cruel, foreign and bloodthirsty oppressors.
   We suffer with all our heart over the multitudinous and excessive cruel violences, the excessive burdens, taxes of ten, twenty and thirty per cent, and other imposts, exactions, burdens, seizures, slayings, expulsions, confiscations, executions and innumerable
10 other unparalleled and intolerable inflictions, intimidations, and oppressions which the common enemy with his Spaniards, bishops, inquisitors and other dependants, continues daily with unprecedented novelty and violence to inflict upon you, your wives and your daughters, and your souls, bodies and goods. After
15 so many years, this now grows steadily worse under the name of His Royal Majesty, but without his knowledge, in violation of his oath, and contrary to the liberties and privileges of the country, although in fact at the instigation of Cardinal Granvelle and the Spanish inquisitors, whose purpose is to put into effect the deci-
20 sions of the Council of Trent and the Inquisition of Spain. These events are so public and well known that I do not need to give any broader account of them.
   You know and the whole world knows with what diligence and cost of money, difficulties and troubles we have worked in order to
25 restore to each and all of you and to our beloved fatherland your former freedom, prosperity and wealth and to deliver you from foreign tyrants and oppressors . . . To achieve this if you will help by giving yourselves over into our hands we wish to contribute all our strength, but if you do not and bring shame, violence and grief
30 upon yourselves, we do not want to have the fault laid upon us.

How is this sudden change in Orange's political aims to be explained? Spanish critics assumed that Orange was cynically buying with promises a body of followers whom he would use to help him regain his lost lands and prestige in the Netherlands. For their part, Orange's own publicists claimed that the Prince had always served his country and that he was now expounding a cause which had long been maturing in his mind. Generally, historians have steered a midway position between these two interpretations. Certainly, after 1567 Orange was desperate for allies and, to win these, he was ready to make all variety of concessions and commitments – even to the extent of changing his religion. On the other hand, there is much to suggest that Orange's own misfortunes had awakened in him a deeper appreciation of the hardships under which his fellow countrymen laboured. The oppressions of Spanish rule weighed heavily on the towns and hamlets of the Netherlands. Orange's own struggle made the estates and townsfolk his natural allies and forged between him and the people of the Netherlands a community of interests and sympathies. Thus, within only a few months of his flight the former leader of the aristocratic opposition was effectively transformed into *Pater Patriae*, the Father of the Fatherland. On Orange's part the change was neither completely cynical nor completely altruistic. It was instead a timely combination of calculation and conviction.

Orange's political methods also changed. To begin with, he worked from within the existing structure so as to change it. Although his strategy between 1559 and 1566 was a dangerous one, he did not espouse violent means nor overtly threaten the ruler and Regent. He worked against the ruler's servants and policies by using the traditional instruments of the disaffected nobleman – whipping up noisy support and whenever possible gaining the ear of the Regent to make his case known. According to the conventions of the day neither Orange nor his fellow grandees had committed any offence by the time of his flight in 1567. Thus, the unwary Egmont and Hornes were astonished at their eventual arrest. Both went to their executions protesting their innocence and affirming their utter loyalty to Philip.

After 1567 Orange's methods were bound to change. He could hardly work 'from within' while in exile. Thus he took up arms and announced his intention to drive the Spaniards out of the Netherlands. Right up to the 1580s, however, Orange maintained that he was not fighting Philip but was struggling against the evil advisers who had misled their master and the Spanish troops whose excesses harmed the King's reputation. During this period little was considered more appalling than making war on one's lawful ruler. Orange had therefore to maintain the fiction that he was still a loyal subject. Hence a song, originally written in 1569, the *Wilhelmus*, which commemorates William of Orange and is the Dutch national anthem, contains Orange's avowal, 'I have always honoured the King of Spain'.

To sustain his rebellion and to keep the allies he had gathered, Orange had to translate the promises he had earlier made into a concrete form. Once he had established the 'bridgehead' in Holland and Zealand, he admitted the estates into a political partnership. But this method of maintaining the commitment of his allies was regarded by Orange as a purely emergency expedient. In his negotiations with foreign rulers for assistance, entered into during the early months of 1576, Orange's proposals for the future government of the Netherlands afforded very little place for the estates. As we will see in the next section, Orange was again ready in the 1580s to restrict the powers of the States-General when this body proved itself ineffective at governing. In brief, Orange was the champion of representative institutions only as long as this cause suited his purpose. For Orange, establishing a partnership with the estates was simply one means of maintaining his influence over political affairs.

The one consistent aim in Orange's career was to protect freedom of conscience. As far as his political ideas and methods are concerned we must carefully distinguish two phrases: before 1566/67 and after. In the first period Orange was reacting to the changes Philip had imposed on the government of the Netherlands and was trying to restore the grandees as the principal advisers to the Regent. After 1567 his concern became the restoration of those more general political rights which Spanish rule had erased. In order to accomplish a Spanish withdrawal he needed allies: hence his readiness to change his religion and to make an accommodation with the provincial estates. As Professor Swart has explained (see Further Reading, page 112), 'Orange was not a doctrinaire revolutionary intent on founding a new political and social order, but a prudent, highly practical and occasionally unscrupulous statesman.'

3 Orange and the Revolt 1577–84

a) Don John

In February 1577 the new Governor-General, Don John of Austria, swore in the Perpetual Edict to maintain the Pacification of Ghent. In May, only a few days after the last Spanish troops had left the Netherlands for Italy, Don John entered Brussels. It was now his task to restore Spanish prestige and authority in the Netherlands.

Don John's orders from Philip were far from specific. Philip recognised that the policy of brute force employed by Alva and Requesens had failed, for Spain could not shoulder the double burden of a war in the Netherlands and in the Mediterranean, where a new Turkish offensive had started. Philip therefore required Don John only 'to save what we can preserving religion and my authority as much as may be.' He recommended that Don John try to work with the political leaders in the Netherlands and accommodate himself 'to Time and Necessity which are the best counsellors you can have.'

Don John realised that Spanish rule could not be restored completely to the Netherlands without the support of William of Orange. Orange had the forces of Holland and Zealand behind him whereas the Spanish army had just left the country. In addition, although the authority of Orange only technically extended to those provinces of which he was the *stadholder* – Holland, Zealand and Utrecht – the Prince had a hard core of followers in the States-General and could through them seriously disrupt the passage of business there. The trouble was that Orange refused to come to terms with Don John. He believed that once Philip had gathered sufficient funds he would order Don John to renew the destruction of Protestantism and of local rights. As he put it to the envoys of Don John, 'We can see that you wish to exterminate us and we do not wish to be exterminated.'

Impatient and frustrated, Don John recalled the Spanish troops in July 1577. His timing was fortuitous, for Philip had just concluded a truce with the Turkish Sultan and was once more free to concentrate all his efforts on the Netherlands. The King, therefore, gave permission for the war to be renewed.

Don John's treachery confirmed that Orange had been right all along to refuse to deal with him. The States-General, in fear of the Spaniards' return, ordered Orange and his troops to come at once to its aid. In September 1577 Orange entered Brussels where he was given a rapturous welcome by the crowds and, a few weeks later, the office of *ruwaard* (governor) of Brabant. No longer was Orange's influence just confined to Holland and Zealand. The faithlessness of Don John had lent Orange prestige and credibility throughout the Netherlands and had raised him to the position of *de facto* leader of his country. Even former rivals of the Prince were now ready to assure him that, 'all our hopes rest on you'.

b) The Unions of Arras and Utrecht

In the autumn of 1577 the opportunity briefly existed for a united front to be set up in the Netherlands under the leadership of the Prince of Orange. However, this opportunity for concerted resistance to Spain evaporated when social and religious strife combined with differing local interests to create disharmony and division.

During the chaos of 1576–77 the guildsmen of Brussels and Ghent had seized power from the patricians who had for so long dominated the political and economic life of the towns. In the wake of these urban revolutions, Calvinist exiles from the north had entered the towns and had begun stirring up the inhabitants against the Catholic faith. By associating Catholicism with the Spanish enemy, the preachers had been able to win converts and allies. Early in 1578 the Calvinists of Ghent marched on neighbouring Oudenaarde, overthrew its council and imposed their own faith on the town. Similar 'revolutions' occurred across Flanders, Brabant and Artois, and were accompanied by iconoclasm and the banning of Catholic worship. Orange tried in vain to impose a religious peace on the troubled regions with a scheme for allowing both religions to be practised unmolested.

* It was the advance of Calvinism into the south which alarmed many of the moderate Catholics and ultimately led to their return to the Spanish fold. However, it was not so much religion as Orange himself, and what he stood for, which drew the grandees of the Netherlands into the enemy's camp. Many of the grandees nursed deep suspicions of the

Prince of Orange and none less than their foremost spokesman, the Duke of Aerschot, whose own family, the House of Croy, had long been a rival of the House of Orange-Nassau. In particular, it was the support which Orange drew from the lower orders and his readiness to advance the authority of the States-General which offended the aristocracy. The grandees were convinced that they alone should administer the Netherlands and they were disdainful of the townsmen and lesser nobles who attended the States-General. Thus they plotted to outmanoeuvre Orange and, when outmanoeuvred themselves, reconciled themselves to the continuation of Spanish rule.

Shortly after Don John's treachery, when it seemed that Orange might be chosen by the States-General as the new governor, the grandees invited the Archduke Matthias, who was Philip's Austrian nephew, to the Netherlands. The Archduke was young and impressionable and the grandees reckoned that he would be a pliant instrument in their hands. At the grandees' bidding the States-General agreed to appoint Matthias governor in place of Don John. The young Archduke arrived in the Netherlands in October 1577.

Orange quickly upset the grandees' calculations. By working through his supporters in the States-General and by mounting demonstrations in the major towns of the south, Orange pushed the States-General into recognising the new governor on condition that he ruled with a Council of State appointed by the delegates. Also, at Orange's behest, the States-General made Matthias accept Orange as his lieutenant and chief adviser. By this second stipulation Matthias was reduced to little more than Orange's cipher. The grandees had been outwitted.

While the debates about the proper relationship of Matthias, Orange and the States-General were going on in Brussels, the Spanish army returned to the Netherlands from Italy. Under the command of the Duke of Parma, Don John's deputy, the Spaniards rapidly put the army of the States-General into retreat, defeating it in January 1578 at Gembloux. This calamity provided, however, a new and unexpected opportunity for the grandees. Under the guise of enlisting friendly foreign help, they realised that they could introduce a 'third force' into the domestic politics of the Netherlands which would operate as a counterweight to Orange. Their choice for this role was Duke Francis of Anjou, the brother of the French King.

In July 1578 Anjou entered the Netherlands at the invitation of Count Lalaing, a leading grandee. The next month the States-General granted the French prince the title 'Defender of the Liberties of the Netherlands'. But at Orange's insistence, Anjou was specifically excluded from any share in the government of the country. His job, he was told, was to fight the Spaniards. For this purpose Anjou agreed to bring 12 000 troops of his own into the war.

★ Anjou's involvement in the affairs of the Netherlands was unwelcome to Elizabeth I of England who feared that the country would become a French satellite. Attempting to restrict Anjou's activities she wooed him, even hinting that she was prepared to marry her 'dear frog', while simultaneously seeking to outmanoeuvre him in military diplomacy. In August 1578 Elizabeth paid for a German mercenary army, led by John Casimir of the Rhineland Palatinate, to enter the Netherlands with orders to assist the States-General. In the negotiations leading up to John Casimir's intervention the Prince of Orange played an influential role, for he hoped that Elizabeth's new interest in the Netherlands would result in her eventually sending an army of her own to assist him.

John Casimir, however, proved less anxious to engage the Spaniards than to assist the Calvinists in their struggle against the Catholics. Having failed to rendezvous with the army of the States-General, John Casimir entered Ghent where his men threw themselves into anti-Catholic excesses. In the mean time, the Calvinists in Holland and Zealand completed their own religious conquest of these provinces by overcoming the Catholic strongholds of Haarlem and Amsterdam. Thereafter, they turned their attention to Utrecht and Gelderland, 'cleansing' these provinces also of Catholic worship.

The activities of John Casimir and the spread of Calvinist revolution were enough to drive many Catholics, who had previously supported the war against Spain, over to the Spanish side. These were joined by many of the moderate members of the provincial estates in the south who were alarmed by the continuing civil disorder. To their number were added the grandees whose own attempts to restrain the influence of Orange had so signally failed. For support these groups increasingly relied on former units of the States-General's army which had mutinied either for lack of pay or in protest at the excesses of the Calvinists. Fighting broke out in October 1578 between the mutineers, or Malcontents as they were known, and the army of John Casimir. Although John Casimir left the Netherlands for good a few months later, the ill-feeling caused by his heavy-handed intervention in the domestic politics of the Netherlands contributed substantially to the division which followed.

* Early in 1579 the three southern provinces of Hainault, Walloon Flanders and Artois, the estates of which were dominated by Catholics and by conservative noblemen, seceded from the States-General and established their own confederation, called the Union of Arras. Immediately representatives of the Union entered into talks with the Duke of Parma, who had succeeded as governor on the death of Don John the previous year. The result of their negotiations was the Peace of Arras wherein the Union recognised the authority of Philip II and of Parma in return for the following concessions:

1 In order to maintain appreciably better confidence among the subjects of His Majesty by means of a good union and accord in the service of God for the preservation of the Roman, Apostolic and Catholic religion, and obedience to His Majesty, together with the

5 repose and prosperity of the country, both parties consent to a
   perpetual amnesty for all things that may have been said or done
   since the beginning of hostilities, or in consequence of them . . .
   His Majesty shall send out all Spanish, Italian, Burgundian and
   other foreign troops not acceptable to the country within six weeks
10 of publication of the present treaty or earlier . . . During the time
   until the departure of the said foreigners, His Majesty and the
   United Lands will raise an army of natives of this country and
   others acceptable to His Majesty and to the estates of the provinces
   . . .
15 His Majesty will choose for his Council of State ten or twelve
   persons, including lords and nobles as well as men of learning, all
   natives of the country, of which two-thirds shall be acceptable to
   the estates of the said provinces . . .
   All correspondence and dispatches shall be drawn up according
20 to the advice and decisions of the councillors of state.
   These provinces shall henceforth not be burdened in any way
   with taxes, tributes or impositions other than those which were in
   force during the time of the late Emperor Charles, and with the
   consent of the estates of each province respectively. Each and all of
25 these shall be maintained in their privileges, usages and customs,
   in general and individually. And in the event that any be infringed,
   it shall be made good and restored.

News of the deliberations going on in the south hastened the formation
of a separate union in the north. In January 1579 deputies from Holland,
Zealand, Friesland, Gelderland and Utrecht met in the town of Utrecht
to set up a rival organisation of their own. Their union, the Union of
Utrecht, was soon extended to include all those provinces which
remained loyal to the States-General. The Netherlands was now split in
two, with a pro-Spanish Catholic grouping in the south and a rebel
organisation in the north. Orange was appalled at this development for
he had always hoped to establish a free and united Netherlands. But
eventually recognising the inevitable, he reconciled himself with the
Union of Utrecht in May 1579.

The Union of Utrecht established a confederation of provinces. It
made no adequate provision for new central institutions so the States-
General continued to act as the main forum for delegates from the
provinces – although of course those from the Arras Union were
excluded from attendance. The articles of the Union upheld the principle
of provincial autonomy, and the signatories agreed that:

1 The aforesaid provinces shall ally, confederate and unite to hold
  together eternally in all ways and forms as if they were but one
  province and they shall not separate from each other . . . However
  this is agreed without prejudice to the special and particular privi-

5   leges, freedoms, exemptions, laws, statutes, laudable and traditional customs, usages and all other rights of each province and of
each town, member and inhabitant of those provinces. Not only
shall the provinces not hinder each other from exercising these
rights nor impair, nor prejudice them in any way, but they shall
10 help each other by all proper and possible means, if necessary with
their lives and with their property, to maintain and strengthen
them, and they shall protect and defend them against all and
everyone who may actually design to encroach upon them.

As far as religious affairs were concerned the treaty of union specified
that:

Concerning the matter of religion, Holland and Zealand shall act at
15 their own discretion, whereas the other provinces of this union may
introduce (all together or each province separately), without being
hindered or prevented from doing this by any other province, such
regulations as they consider proper for the peace and welfare of the
provinces, towns and their particular members and for the preser-
20 vation of all people, either secular or clerical, their properties and
rights, provided that in accordance with the Pacification of Ghent
each individual enjoys freedom of religion and no one is persecuted
or questioned about his religion . . .
The deputies who are responsible for and have concluded this
25 union declare that it has never been and is not now their purpose
and intention to exclude from the union and alliance any towns or
provinces which want to maintain the Catholic religion exclusively
. . . For it is not their opinion that one province or town should lay
down the law to others in the matter of religion, as they want to
30 further peace and unity among the provinces and to avoid and take
away the main occasion for quarrels and discord.

The hopes expressed in this document that Catholic worship would be
respected were not fulfilled. As the loyal Catholics in the provinces of the
Union of Utrecht either left for the south or were shouldered out of
positions of leadership, the provincial estates one by one passed restrictions on Catholic worship. However, in the 1580s, Calvinism was still a
minority religion followed by scarcely ten per cent of the population in
the provinces of the Union. But the minority were noisy, organised and
had the local estates behind them. Thus violent attacks on Catholic
places of worship, schools and religious houses continued. Vainly did
Orange recommend a policy of forbearance and a régime which allowed
freedom of worship to all. He was told that 'a man cannot be a good
patriot and a papist'.

4 The Duke of Anjou

Meanwhile in the south the process of Spanish reconquest had begun. Led by Parma, who discovered that the rebel commanders were not averse to changing sides if sufficient money was offered, armies supplied by the Union of Arras retook Maastricht and s'Hertogenbosch in 1579 and Breda and Courtrai in the following year. In a slow pincer movement Parma's troops advanced up into Brabant while from Groningen they began moving into the far north towards Holland. By the early 1580s it seemed that Parma was unstoppable.

The failure of the rebels to slow Parma's advance resulted from the extreme disorganisation of the Union of Utrecht. The Union was essentially an alliance of provinces acting independently. No effective government had been appointed at the centre to coordinate political and military affairs. For its part, the States-General was no more than the meeting place in which delegates from the separate provinces communicated the views of the local estates, seldom reaching a consensus. As Orange lamented, 'Everyone in his own province or town acts as he thinks beneficial to himself.' In short, the term 'United Provinces', as the member-provinces of the Utrecht Union styled their collective organisation, was a misnomer, better the expression 'Disunited Provinces'.

Orange's solution to the grievous lack of centralised direction was the appointment of a sovereign ruler. The Archduke Matthias would have been one possibility for this role had he not already demonstrated his feeble grasp of political affairs – he finally left the Netherlands in 1581. Orange's attention fastened on the Duke of Anjou. Anjou was of royal birth (regarded at the time a precondition of sovereignty) and had in the recent French civil wars shown reasonable intelligence. He could also bring in French help for the United Provinces and Orange was convinced that the native armies were insufficient to restrain Parma's advance. Furthermore, Anjou was a Catholic and Orange hoped that his appointment as sovereign would help stem the tide of Calvinist intolerance.

During 1580 and 1581 Orange's scheme was pushed through the States-General by his supporters. Firstly, Anjou was offered the title 'Prince and Lord of the Netherlands'. Then, once Anjou had accepted this office, King Philip was in July 1581 solemnly deposed by the States-General as ruler of the Netherlands. In August Anjou arrived with an army of 17 000 Frenchmen and immediately set about relieving the towns under siege by Parma. Early the next month, he was invested with the title of Duke of Brabant – and it was Orange who fastened the ermine cloak of office to his shoulders during the splendid ceremony.

However, the grand gestures which attended Anjou's entry to the Netherlands proved empty symbols. He was unable to curb the excesses of the local Calvinists and was disturbed to see the humiliation of his own Catholic faith. In addition, the estates of Holland and Zealand refused to recognise his sovereignty and declared that they preferred Orange as their lord. Finally, the States-General hedged Anjou's authority with all sorts of limitations and restrictions, binding him to govern only in consultation with the deputies. Anjou's pride was unable to withstand these insults. In January 1583 he tried in a military coup to seize the power that had been denied him. When this failed, he left the Netherlands, dying in France the next year.

Anjou's death was rapidly followed by Orange's own. In March 1580 Philip had declared Orange an outlaw and had put a price on his head. Orange replied in a lengthy document, known as the *Apology*, in which he justified his past actions and accused the King of tyranny. Orange's arguments did not convince a certain Balthasar Gérard, for whom the Catholic faith and the prospect of a pocketful of money carried more weight. On Tuesday 10 July 1584, Balthasar using a false identity was admitted to Orange's presence. Suddenly producing a pistol, he fired point-blank.

Orange fell with his life's work in ruins before him. The Netherlands was divided and the enemy was fast encroaching on the part which remained free. Religious tolerance had not been won – neither in the south where Catholicism remained the exclusive faith, nor in the north where Calvinism had established itself as the only public religion. Orange's chosen method of partnership with the estates had similarly failed. In the United Provinces the States-General was riven by arguments and Orange's latest bid to establish stronger military and political direction had, thanks to Anjou, proved unsuccessful. Orange's last words provide fitting testimony to the serious plight in which his untimely death left his countrymen: 'God have pity on my soul and on this poor people.'

Making notes on William of Orange and the Revolt, 1576–84

The following activities, headings and questions should help you. Read sections 1 and 2 of the chapter and make brief notes under these headings:

1.   Orange's position in 1576
2.   The aims of William of Orange
2.1.   Orange and religion
2.2.   Political aims and methods

Make two lists of evidence, one to support the interpretation that Orange was motivated by principle and one to support the interpretation that his actions can be explained in terms of expediency. Explain where the truth, in your opinion, lies.

3.   Orange and the Revolt, 1577–84

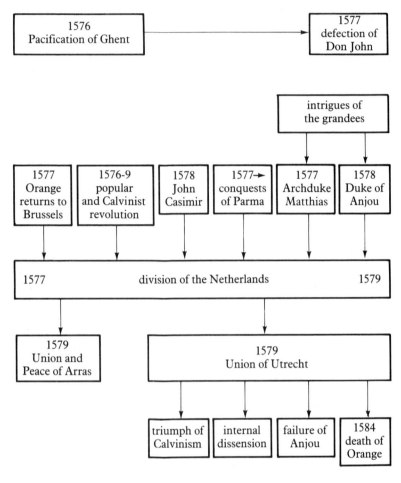

Summary – William of Orange and the Revolt, 1576–84

Go through sections 3 and 4 of the chapter. Make a chronological list of
events. Give each event a date and a name, and explain in one sentence

the significance of the event in terms of the three-cornered struggle between Philip II, the loyal grandees, and William of Orange and his supporters.

Look back in your notes to 2.1. and 2.2. Consider how many, or how few, of Orange's aims had been fulfilled by the time of his death in 1584. Make two lists, one of fulfilled aims and one of unfulfilled aims.

Answering essay questions on 'William of Orange'

William of Orange is an old chestnut regularly brought out of the fire for A-level examinations. Questions on Orange are usually undemanding and straightforward:

'Examine the aims and methods of William the Silent.'

However, in approaching this type of generalised biographical question, you should at all costs avoid writing a chronological narrative. Do not even give a potted version at the start of your essay; it will earn no marks. Make your plan by completing half a dozen sentences beginning 'One of Orange's aims was . . .'. Avoid vague statements such as 'to set the Netherlands free', and distinguish in your own mind between aims and methods.

You will need at the start of your essay to state clearly that Orange's plans changed along with the course of the Revolt. Hereafter, make it obvious to the reader at what point in his career Orange had the objectives you are ascribing to him. Otherwise, the reader will get in a muddle and think you are muddled instead. Remember! Historians like dates not because they are fond of numbers but because, if they are to understand the processes of change, cause and effect, they have to be aware of the correct sequence in which events take place. For this reason it is always better to give an approximate date than no date at all.

As an alternative to 'aims and methods', you may be asked to make an overall assessment of Orange's career:

'What was the contribution of William of Orange to the Revolt of the Netherlands?'

'What had William of Orange achieved by the time of his death in 1584?'

For these questions you will need to consider Orange's role in the events and intrigues of 1559–67, and the extent to which he was responsible for the uprising in 1566. His actions between 1567 and 1572 should be dealt with briefly, although a case can be made that the new political aims he adopted at this time broadened the appeal, and thus the potency, of the Revolt. Orange's defence of Holland and Zealand between 1572 and 1576 and his role in securing the Pacification should be mentioned. But devote the main part of your analysis to 1576–84. Discuss Orange's promotion of the States-General into the main instrument of government, and his opposition to the machinations of Don John and the grandees which ensured that the previous gains of the Revolt were not compromised. In the final paragraph of the essay, present a brief summary of your findings beginning, 'The contribution/achievement of William of Orange was therefore to have . . .'

Do remember that William of Orange may alternatively be called William the Silent, although the reasons for this nickname are obscure. There are cases of A-level candidates not only believing William the Silent to be somebody other than William of Orange but also putting these two figures on opposing sides!

Source-based questions on 'William of Orange'

1 William of Orange
Read the extract from Orange's autobiography on page 42, and the text of the letter he wrote in 1572 (page 44). Answer the following questions:
a)   What reasons does Orange give in the autobiographical extract for his early commitment to drive the Spaniards out of the Netherlands?
b)   What additional reasons does Orange give in his letter of 1572 for opposing the present system of Spanish rule in the Netherlands?
c)   Why in the letter of 1572 might Orange suggest that the horrors he enumerates were happening without the knowledge of the King?
d)   How far do these two documents suggest that Orange's principal aim was to restore the rights and privileges which an innovatory Spanish government had erased? Do you find this suggestion convincing?

2 The Unions of Arras and Utrecht
Read the extract from the terms of the Peace of Arras, given on pages 49–50, and the extracts from the articles of the Union of Utrecht on pages 50–51. Answer the following questions:
a)   What light does the extract taken from the Peace of Arras throw upon the aims of those parties which had joined the Union of Arras?
b)   What two things did Philip II gain in return for agreeing to the concessions enumerated in the Peace of Arras?
c)   How do the religious terms of the Peace of Arras differ from those laid down in the articles of the Union of Utrecht?

d) What aims did the signatories to the Union of Utrecht share in common with the Netherlanders who agreed to the Peace of Arras?

e) The articles of the Union of Utrecht specified that the constituent provinces would in future act 'as if they were but one province'. To what extent do the clauses which follow reveal this commitment to be a hollow one?

CHAPTER 4

The Revolt 1584–1609

1 Parma and Maurice

Orange's death in 1584 did not put an end to the resistance to Spain. For the next 25 years the United Provinces continued the struggle and, although the rebels did not recapture the southern provinces, Spain was eventually forced in 1609 to call a truce. Spanish failure to crush the rebels may be ascribed to a variety of factors. In this section, the conflict will be analysed from a strictly military point of view: in terms of leadership, strategy, allies and discipline. In the next section, the influence of political organisation and of economic resources on the eventual outcome of the war will be separately considered.

Duke Alexander Farnese of Parma, son of the former regent of the Netherlands, had arrived in the country in 1577 as Don John's lieutenant. The next year, on Don John's death, Parma had taken over as governor. In strict accordance with the Peace of Arras, the terms of which are explained in the preceding chapter, Parma had withdrawn the Spanish forces in 1579 and had continued the war against the United Provinces with native troops. Although these were ill-disciplined, Parma had still managed to overrun much of the territory occupied by his enemies. However, Parma had realised that his triumphs owed much to the internal disorganisation of the United Provinces. Should the north coordinate its military affairs, then the tide of events might be turned.

Between 1579 and 1583 Parma had worked hard to establish the two essential preconditions for the reconquest of the north: cash and reliable troops. Early in 1582 he had convinced the leaders of the southern provinces that the south would eventually fall unless the Spanish troops were recalled. That summer, 60 000 had arrived from Italy. They were in Parma's words, 'veteran troops, well-disciplined, born to suffer and to fight against the Netherlanders'. At the same time Parma had extracted from Philip a promise that the Spanish army in the Netherlands would be promptly and regularly paid. Parma had not been prepared to have the fruits of victory stolen by mutiny.

With the troops of Spain now at his command Parma had put into effect in 1583 his strategy for reconquest. His plan was to occupy the Flemish coastline and blockade the Scheldt. He intended by so doing to undermine the economies of the towns of Brabant and Flanders and cut off their supply routes to the north, thus forcing their surrender. Parma's strategy had been so successful that by 1584 all Flanders had been occupied. Antwerp itself had been put under siege, finally surrendering in August 1585. By the year's end all the great towns of Brabant had surrendered.

After 1585, though, Parma's advance slackened. Holland, Zealand,

Utrecht and Friesland remained uncaptured, together with most of Gelderland. From these provinces a counter-offensive was begun in the 1590s which undid much of Parma's earlier work. By the opening years of the seventeenth century the United Provinces had expanded to include Groningen and Overijssel – thus making seven provinces in all – and small slices of Brabant and Flanders. Spanish rule was thus confined to the ten provinces which made up the southern half of the Netherlands.

Both the success of the Spanish army in the early 1580s and its failure to carry through the complete reconquest of the Netherlands may be partly explained by the relative strengths of Spanish and rebel military organisation. During the 1580s the Spanish troops were led by a general of ability and imagination. By contrast, their foes suffered from contra-dictory orders and a poor command structure. During the 1590s this circumstance was reversed. In 1592 Parma died. Two rival commanders, the Count of Fuentes and Count Mansfelt, took Parma's place and the Brussels government became characterised more by bickering than by purposeful leadership. In contrast, over the same period, the supreme command of the rebel forces was attached to one man, Maurice of Nassau, the son of William of Orange. Appointed commander in 1587, Maurice was able to coordinate strategy in the north. Like the Duke of Parma he proved to be a military leader of ability and of inventive skill.

* As Alva had discovered 20 years before, the terrain of the north Netherlands gave substantial benefit to defenders. The lakes and bogs slowed invading forces while the great rivers of the region, although not providing an impregnable barrier, hindered movement. The presence of a large number of fortified towns also consumed an invader's time as each had to be besieged.

Maurice deployed his resources in such a way as to take maximum advantage of the physical geography of the north. He made use of smaller units which allowed for flexibility in harrassing the enemy. At the same time he made sure that his army did not become disunited. Equipment was standardised and distributed by a system of supply-depots; disci-pline was instilled by proper military training, and the number of officers was increased. In reading the works of classical authors, Maurice learned of the art of manoeuvre as against the art of battle which was just the type of strategy suited to the type of fighting in which he was engaged. To protect the northern provinces against the Spanish armies, Maurice reinforced the fortifications of the border-towns. During the early years of the seventeenth century, he built a line of fortifications which was designed to complement the natural barrier across the Netherlands formed by the great rivers.

* Maurice received much support from Elizabeth I of England. In 1585 the Queen, who was alarmed at Parma's successes in the Nether-lands, decided to end her policy of neutrality and signed the Treaty of Nonsuch with the rebels. She agreed to send 7000 English troops to the Netherlands and to lend the States-General enough money to maintain

them. At first the arrangement did not prosper. The English commander, the Earl of Leicester, proved incompetent. He resigned in 1588, by
which time the English army had drifted into mutiny and its officers into
treason. Leicester's successors proved more capable. Sir Francis Vere
assisted Maurice in nearly all the great campaigns of the 1590s, contributing both daring and expertise to the counter offensive. Subordinate to
Vere was a group of able and loyal English commanders: Williams,
Morgan and Norris. As one historian of Anglo-Dutch relations has
observed, had Elizabeth chosen to support the rebels earlier on, the
north might not just have been preserved but the rebels might have
conquered all the southern provinces as well.

   * In contrast to the single-mindedness Maurice and his English allies
displayed, Parma and his successors were obliged by the King of Spain to
divert their energies away from the north. In 1588 Parma was ordered to
hold back his troops from a new offensive so that they could be ready to
support the Armada against England. Two years later, Philip instructed
Parma to enter France and support the forces of the French Catholic
League in their war against Henry IV. Within a few months Parma was in
Paris – and the rebels had recaptured Breda. So appalled was Parma at
the King's decision to subordinate the war against the United Provinces
to campaigning in France that in 1591 he refused the royal order to march
once more against Henry IV. Only Parma's death in 1592 prevented his
arrest on charges of disobedience.

   Part of the reason for Parma's early successes against the rebels lay in
the financial strength of the Brussels government. Until 1587 Philip
stood by his promise to Parma that the Spanish troops in the Netherlands
would be regularly paid. Hereafter, though, the fitting-out of the
Armada and the war against Henry IV of France consumed the major
share of the Spanish finances. As a consequence the army in the Nether
lands was left unpaid. A spate of mutinies began in 1589: the first of over
40 during the period to 1607. Because of the confusion of the Spanish
forces, Maurice was able to achieve substantial victories. The area north
of the River Maas fell to Maurice between 1591 and 1594 largely because
the Spanish garrisons were in revolt. Groningen was conquered in 159
for the same reason. In 1600 the fruits of the previous year's successful
offensive were even sold to the rebels by Spanish mutineers in return for
a settlement of their wages! Back in the 1570s the governor-general
Requesens had complained that the Netherlands would be lost not by the
activities of the rebels but by the 'soldiers born in Valladolid and Toledo'
who disobeyed their commanders and became mutineers. The behaviour
of the Spanish army in the 1590s and early 1600s substantially confirmed
Requesens' warning.

2 The United Provinces and the Spanish Provinces

In the early years of the seventeenth century an English visitor to the

Netherlands made the following observations on the wealth and good government of the United Provinces which he contrasted with the poverty and decay of the southern or 'Spanish' provinces:

1   The care [shown by the north Netherlanders] in government is very exact and precise, because everyone has an immediate interest in the state. Such is the equality of justice here that every man is satisfied; with such care are regulations drawn up that a man may
5   see the laws as a guide, not a means of entrapment; such their exactness in calculating the expense of an army, as that it shall be equally free from superfluity and want . . .
    The largest part of the income of the United Provinces comes from trade, in which business they are nowadays the wisest. For all the
10 commodities that this part of the world wants, and the Indies have (as spices, silk, jewels, gold), they convey – as the Venetians did of old. And all those commodities that the northern Baltic countries abound with and the southern countries stand in need of, they likewise convey thither, which was the ancient trade of the Easter-
15 lings [Germans]. And this they do, having little export of their own, buying and selling at their own prices.
    As soon as I entered the southern country, I beheld the results of a land distressed by war. The people forlorn, and more reproachful of their governors than revengeful against their enemies. The
20 bravery of what was left of the nobility and the industry of the merchants were both decayed. The towns were ruinous and the people here were growing poor with less taxes than they seem to flourish with in the United Provinces.

In the last section the military background to the United Provinces' successful resistance to the Spanish armies was discussed. There are, however, as the above passage suggests, deeper reasons for the failure of the Spanish reconquest: namely, the growing economic strength of the United Provinces and the establishment there, during the 1590s, of an orderly government. These developments may be contrasted with the situation in the south where the local economy was in tatters and where the government was enfeebled by its dependence on Spain.
    In 1596 Philip II appointed his Austrian nephew, the Archduke Albert, governor-general of the Netherlands. On Philip's death in 1598, Albert was granted full sovereignty over the Spanish provinces and, shortly afterwards, he married the late King's daughter, Isabella. Although the joint-rule of 'the Archdukes', as they were known, lasted until 1621, Albert and Isabella remained beholden to Philip III, Philip II's son and successor, for cash and troops. In this way the Spanish King was able to exercise a strong influence over the policy of the court in Brussels, while all military decisions continued to be made in Madrid.
    The government of the Archdukes was highly centralised. Under their

rule the provincial estates were reduced to little more than tax-raising assemblies; in the towns power was entrusted to groups of patricians who took their instructions from the Archdukes. A wide range of arbitrary powers allowed the Archdukes' government to override local rights and established procedures. In Brussels itself, the Council of State, on which the leaders of the Catholic nobility sat, was rendered less than even an advisory body, for the advice of the Council was seldom asked. Decisions were made instead by 'the Spanish ministry', which was an informal body of Spaniards. As the grandees gave up the capital and drifted back to their country estates, the court of the Archdukes assumed an increasingly foreign and alien air. One observer remarked of Archduke Albert, 'He imitates the government of Philip II as closely as possible and conforms in everything to the usages of the Spanish court.'

* The provinces over which the Archdukes ruled had been the battleground of the Netherlands since 1572. Thirty years of warfare had sapped their economic vitality. Trade was disrupted and industry was destroyed by the fighting. After 1585 a blockade of the Scheldt estuary by the armies of the United Provinces destroyed what was left of Antwerp's commerce. A flight of manpower and capital from south to north contributed also to economic decline. Between 1570 and 1600 the population of Antwerp fell by a third; that of Louvain and Mechlin by a half. Even though recovery came during the first decades of the seventeenth century, it was insufficient to restore the provinces to prosperity.

By the early years of the seventeenth century Spain was neither capable of sustaining the war in the Netherlands nor of funding the government of the Spanish provinces. In 1596 the Spanish crown declared a state bankruptcy. In 1607 Philip III repudiated his own debts. As a result the amount of money paid by Spain to the Brussels government diminished every year. Because of the ravaged economic condition of the south, local taxation was insufficient to make up the shortfall. Not surprisingly, the troops were left unpaid with the consequence of yet more mutinies.

* Meanwhile in the United Provinces a governmental and economic transformation was underway. During the 1580s there had been a major crisis of authority and leadership in the north. The one figure who could have imposed order on the squabbling provincial delegations – the Prince of Orange – was assassinated in 1584. After Orange's death a number of attempts were made to promote a new leader. In 1586 the commander of the English forces in the Netherlands, the Earl of Leicester, was sworn in as 'Absolute Governor'. The States-General gave him full command of military affairs and the right to appoint all public officials. Holland and Zealand, though, were unwilling to follow the Absolute Governor's instructions while Leicester himself proved inept as both a politician and a military commander. In 1588 he left the Netherlands for good and once more the States-General found itself forced to assume the mantle of leadership.

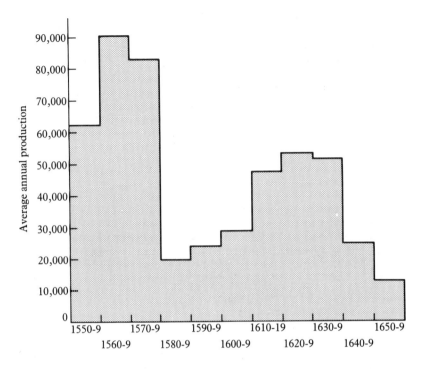

Hondschoote in Flanders; production of serge cloth for export (in 'pieces'), 1550–1659

In the years following Leicester's departure a greater measure of cohesion was achieved in the political organisation of the United Provinces. Between 1585 and 1592 Maurice of Nassau, William of Orange's son, was recognised by the States-General as the *stadholder* of Holland, Zealand, Utrecht, Gelderland and Overijssel. Maurice's cousin and close colleague, William Louis of Nassau, was in turn appointed *stadholder* of Friesland and Groningen. Unity was achieved therefore through the House of Orange in the administrative and military affairs of the United Provinces. Meanwhile, the States-General changed from being a noisy debating chamber into a business-like committee. During the 1590s the provincial estates ceased sending large delegations to attend meetings of the States-General and started despatching just a single representative or 'Advocate'. The advocates still took their instructions from the provincial estates and had to report back to them. But as only a handful of spokesmen usually attended the States-General, agreement could be reached more swiftly than before. Indeed, in pressing matters the States-General sometimes dispensed entirely with the procedure of reporting back to the provincial estates.

Throughout the 1580s the issue of sovereignty troubled the States-General. Monarchy was still regarded the most natural form of government, but in 1581 Philip had been deposed and no lasting replacement had since been found. Anjou had proved a failure while, later on, Elizabeth of England and Henry III of France both turned down offers of sovereignty. The States-General therefore decided to assume 'collective sovereignty' itself and no longer to seek to promote an individual to a position of supreme lordship. In 1590 the States-General declared itself 'the sovereign institution of the country', with complete responsibility for the present and future government of the United Provinces. The United Provinces became therefore a republic, and since its territory consisted mainly of Dutch speakers the United Provinces may also be called 'the Dutch Republic'.

Although the States-General claimed to be the sovereign institution of the country, it conceded that authority ultimately rested not with itself but with the provincial estates. For it was the provincial estates which appointed the advocates who attended the States-General almost as the ambassadors of their respective localities. Thus the United Provinces remained, as its name suggests, a union of separate provinces. Power was decentralised and shared between the component parts of the new republic.

Within the States-General itself direction was increasingly given by the Advocate of Holland, Johan van Oldenbarnevelt. Throughout the 1590s and the first two decades of the next century, Oldenbarnevelt took the lead in the making of policy. It was he, for instance, who urged the States-General to recognise Maurice of Nassau as *stadholder* of five of the provinces. In 1602 the Advocate of Holland was also the architect of the Dutch East India Company, a maritime commercial organisation.

Oldenbarnevelt was also instrumental in establishing the new religious order in the United Provinces. As we have seen, during the 1570s and 1580s the town governments and provincial estates of the north Netherlands were taken over by a minority of Calvinist sympathisers who then imposed restrictions on Catholic worship. However, the local Protestant leaders were not on the whole zealous adherents of the reformed faith. They belonged to the latitudinarian or 'libertinist' wing of Protestantism rather than to its 'strict' branch. The civic leaders encountered opposition in the towns from religious councils and preachers who believed that the Calvinist church hierarchy should be allowed greater control of public affairs. Naturally the town dignitaries resisted this demand since they did not wish to forfeit their authority. Oldenbarnevelt assisted the townsmen in their struggle. He ensured that town councils were allowed the right to dismiss troublesome ministers and made all churchmen in Holland swear oaths of allegiance to the local authorities.

The rise of Oldenbarnevelt may be partly explained by his formidable intellect and tenacity of purpose. However, to a rather greater extent,

Oldenbarnevelt's influence derived from the economic power of Holland, of which province he was the advocate. In this respect, it is no coincidence that from the 1580s the States-General of the United Provinces met in The Hague, the capital of Holland.

* The reconquest of the southern Netherlands by the Duke of Parma was accompanied by the mass exodus of Calvinists. In the following decades the Archdukes permitted Protestants to choose exile instead of imprisonment and death. So successful was this device that by 1609 virtually no Calvinist congregations remained in the south. Most of the refugees went north and became citizens of the United Provinces. Because the eastern and southern flanks of the Republic were war zones, the newcomers mainly settled in Holland and in the coastal towns. In some places the population quadrupled as a consequence of their immigration.

Besides their expertise, particularly in textile manufacture, the immigrants brought their capital. In the past capital had usually been put into land, since property besides keeping its value yielded a regular income from rents. However, in the waterlogged province of Holland land was scarce while the rapid growth of the population had the result of forcing up property prices. The newcomers accordingly sought alternative outlets for investment.

Firstly, wealth was channelled into state loans. The government desperately needed cash to fund the war against Spain. The United Provinces' expenditure on the armed forces rose from 3.2 million florins in 1592 to 8.8 million in 1607. A part of these costs was met by taxation which by the end of the 1590s had become heavier than under Alva. As an alternative to putting up taxes even more, the government raised loans. Since state-bonds yielded an annual interest rate of ten per cent they proved an attractive investment for those with spare capital as well as a ready method for meeting military expenditure.

A second outlet for capital was investment in private enterprises. Land reclamation schemes and industrial ventures both gained from the quantity of wealth available for borrowing. Since investors also put their money into shipping and trade, commercial enterprises benefited. During the last decades of the sixteenth century the Dutch steadily took over the carrying of commodities from the Baltic to Spain (regardless of the war between this country and their own) and into the Mediterranean. Grain, timber and salt were the principal wares which the Dutch traded. In addition, the Dutch purchased wool in Spain, sold it in Holland where it was made into textiles, and then resold the finished product back in Spanish ports.

Although rather less significant than the Baltic–South European trade, commercial routes in the Atlantic and the Pacific were opened up by Dutch shipping, mainly from Rotterdam and Amsterdam. In 1598–99 the first Dutch ship circumnavigated the globe and a Rotterdam sea-captain returned from Indonesia with a valuable cargo of spices. As one observer wrote, 'So long as Holland has been Holland, such richly-laden ships have never been seen.' The sea-captain's success inspired others and over the following years Dutch traders expanded their activities to include the Moluccas, the Philippines, Malaya, Sri Lanka and India. In 1602 a monopoly of the Pacific trade was given to the Dutch East India Company, in the formation of which Oldenbarnevelt played a leading role. The Company was founded with private capital totalling 6½ million florins and raised in just a month – which is a comment in itself on the capital resources and sophistication of investment methods in the United Provinces.

 * By the early years of the seventeenth century, Spain could no longer sustain the war in the Netherlands. Philip III was bankrupt and, after a brief attempt at the start of his reign to make himself a successful warrior-king, he realised his financial limitations. Meanwhile in the United Provinces the hope that the south could still be reconquered gradually receded. An unsuccessful Dutch invasion of Flanders in 1600 revealed that the south was not after all filled with a population eager to throw off the Spanish yoke. Four years later England made peace with Spain, leaving the Republic to stand alone against Philip III. For his part, Oldenbarnevelt had become convinced of the need for peace. A cessation of hostilities would, he reckoned, lessen the tax-burden in the north and provide additional opportunities for commercial expansion. His arguments won over the States-General. In 1607 both sides agreed to an armistice. Two years later the ceasefire was extended in the Truce of Antwerp for a further 12 years.

Making notes on *'The Revolt 1584–1609'*

The following headings and questions should help you:

1.   Parma and Maurice
1.1. Parma's preparations and strategy
1.2. Maurice of Nassau
1.3. English aid
1.4. Diversions and mutinies
How far was the failure of the Spanish armies to subdue the north caused by a) Spanish military weaknesses, and b) Dutch military superiority?
2.   The United Provinces and the Spanish Provinces
2.1. The Archdukes
2.2. The economy of the Spanish provinces
2.3. The government of the United Provinces
2.4. The prosperity of the United Provinces
2.5. The Truce of Antwerp
List the principal religious, governmental and economic differences between the Dutch Republic and the Spanish provinces.

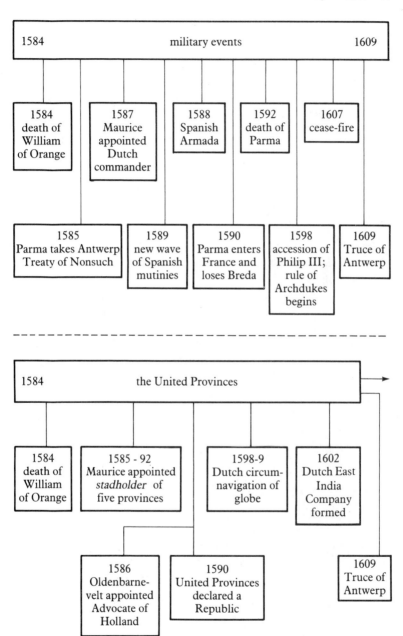

Summary – Military events and the United Provinces, 1584–1609

Answering essay-questions on 'The Revolt 1584–1609'

Essay-questions on this period often ask you to explain why the United Provinces were able to remain independent of Spain. The basis for your answer is provided in the preceding chapter, although you might also like to include points made in the final section of the Analysis (Chapter 5) in order to gain additional information on the problems faced by Spain. Your answer should include material on the military components of Dutch success, on the prosperity of the United Provinces, on the Republic's increasingly efficient method of government and on Spanish weaknesses. Allocate roughly equal space in your essay to each of these factors; do not write so much on one that all the others become crowded into a single paragraph.

An obvious danger in explaining the successful resistance of the United Provinces is that you will exaggerate Dutch strengths and Spanish weaknesses to such an extent that the survival of the Spanish provinces will seem incredible. If the Dutch were so powerful and the Spanish so feeble, why could not the ten southern provinces be 'liberated' also? This thought is anticipated in such questions as:

'Why did just seven provinces of the Netherlands succeed in breaking free of Spanish rule?'

'How do you explain the success of the seven northern provinces of the Netherlands in winning their independence while the ten southern provinces remained under Spanish rule?'

In answering these questions you will need to play down the degree of Spanish weakness and of Dutch might. Consider what limitations the Dutch experienced and what hidden strengths may have been available to Spain. Some points you might include are: Parma's leadership and his strategy of reconquest; the continued commitment of the King of Spain to the struggle; and the removal of potential sources of opposition in the south – what was the lesson of the 1600 campaign in Flanders? In addition you should mention the readiness of the Dutch by the early years of the seventeenth century to give up their attempts to free the southern provinces and make a truce with Spain. Include also the point that English aid may have arrived too late.

Source based questions on 'The Revolt, 1584–1609'

1 The Netherlands, 1584–1609
Read the description of the Netherlands on page 61 and look at the graph reproduced on page 63. Answer the following questions:

a) Explain what is meant by 'everyone has an immediate interest in the state' and 'a man may see the laws as a guide not as a means of entrapment' (lines 2–5). What light do these expressions shed upon the political and constitutional organisation of the United Provinces?

b) How does the author account for the economic prosperity of the United Provinces? Do you find his explanations convincing?

c) What elements of decline does the author identify in his description of the Spanish provinces?

d) To what extent does the graph showing serge-cloth production at Hondschoote confirm the author's contention that distress in the south was primarily the consequence of war?

CHAPTER 5

The Revolt Analysed

How many Revolts?

The various schools of historians have interpreted the Revolt very differently. Nationalist Dutch historians have made the Revolt a patriotic rebellion against Spanish rule. They have concentrated on the great events of 1566, 1572 and 1579 and have explained the part played by William of Orange and Maurice of Nassau as 'founders of the Dutch nation'. By contrast, Belgian historians have focused on the actions of the Catholic nobility and have done their best to rehabilitate the grandees. Meanwhile, Calvinist historians have depicted the revolt as a religious uprising which culminated in a Protestant republic in the north. Marxists have for their part concentrated on the role of the towns and have charted the course of a bourgeois or middle-class revolt. All these interpretations share a common purpose: to portray the events of 1559–1609 as following logically on from one another so as to reach a predetermined conclusion, which may be either a Dutch or Belgian or Calvinist or capitalist state.

During the 1930s Pieter Geyl, a Dutch historian, challenged the notion of there being any completeness to the period 1559–1609. Geyl argued that while the Revolt was primarily a nationalist, anti-Spanish one, it was unable to reach its natural conclusion – the formation of a united and independent Netherlands state – because of Parma's intervention. The reconquest of the 1580s divided the Netherlands along an arbitrary military frontier. More recently, an English historian, Geoffrey Parker, has argued that the Revolt properly consisted of three revolts: a political and religious one in 1566–67; a rebellion against Alva's rule in 1572; and a third uprising in 1576 as a consequence of the Spanish mutinies.

* A quite different method of interpretation has been adopted by Professor J. W. Smit of Columbia University (see Further Reading, page 113) who completely discards any narrative-based approach to the Revolt. Smit sees neither a single revolt nor even a series of consecutive revolts but instead, 'a number of revolts representing the interests and the ideals of various social, economical and ideological groups: revolts which sometimes run parallel, sometimes conflict with one another, and at other times coalesce into a single movement.' Whether or not we agree with Smit's argument, it is certain that his type of analysis identifies most clearly the dynamic forces within the Revolt.

The origins of the Revolt may be traced back to the 'revolt of the grandees' which began with their conspiracy against Granvelle. As described in Chapter 2, Philip II had challenged the aristocracy by denying them a voice in his government in Brussels and by having the

Regent rule through Granvelle and the inner council. The leading grand-ees, Egmont, Hornes and Orange, sought to regain influence for them-selves and for the Council of State, which was the traditional instrument of aristocratic rule; hence their battle against Granvelle. With the impo-sition of Alva's rule the aristocracy were temporarily thwarted. Egmont and Hornes were beheaded; Orange fled; and leadership of the grandees was assumed by such figures as Aerschot and Lalaing, who preferred to play a passive role under Alva and Requesens. Only in the political vacuum which followed Requesens' death did the grandees manage to regain control of the government, although they soon found themselves unequal to the task. Having failed to outmanoeuvre Orange, they turned to the Duke of Parma who in the Peace of Arras promised to give them what they wanted: a share in running the country. Despite Parma's undertaking, the aristocracy soon found itself excluded from influence in the south by the Archduke's 'Spanish ministry'.

During the 1560s the grandees led by Orange combined their chal-lenge to the regent with a plea for the heresy laws to be relaxed. The grandees' intrusion into the religious sphere prompted in turn the for-mation of the Compromise and the confederates' open challenge to the Brussels government. Usually the noblemen who joined the confederates are thought to have been inspired by a mixture of religious concern and anti-Spanish feeling. In fact, recent research has demonstrated that bonds of family and clientage, whereby individuals felt obliged to follow the direction of their feudal lord, drew the confederates close to the leading aristocrats. It is therefore possible that the Compromise was just a device of the grandees, set up and developed to further their own ambitions.

Whatever the circumstances of the confederates' rebellion, following its suppression the nobles were spent as a political force. About a third of the confederates suffered execution, banishment, imprisonment or death in battle in 1567 and the years immediately following. While some of those dispossessed of their lands drifted into brigandage or the ranks of the Sea Beggars, the remainder either sought protection from a powerful feudal overlord or found employment in the service of the state. Thus as a social group the noblemen merged into the small landowning squirear-chy and the bureaucracy. In this respect, their fate may be compared with that of the imperial knights in the Holy Roman Empire.

In the towns a considerable variety of social forces may be perceived. At the top of the urban hierarchy were the wealthy merchants and financiers who dominated the municipal councils and formed the class of patricians. The patricians were above all anxious to preserve political leadership in their respective communities. So they resented Spanish rule since it imposed restraints on their political independence. In the 1580s and for much the same reason, the patricians viewed with alarm the growing political influence of the Calvinist church in the United Provinces and they worked with Oldenbarnevelt to restrict the activities of pastors and synods. Equally, the patricians feared popular disturbances which might spill over into urban revolution. During the Iconoclast Fury of 1566, the leading townsmen held aloof, anxious not to infuriate the crowds by ordering out the local militias. In 1572 the rulers of the towns of Holland and Zealand allowed in the Sea Beggars in order to forestall rebellion among the lower classes. In the southernmost provinces the patricians joined with the local Catholic and Spanish forces during 1578–79 to protect themselves from the sort of guild-led insurrection which had overthrown the town councils of Ghent and Brussels.

On the whole the leading townsmen played a passive role. They did not take positive action such as leading a middle-class or bourgeois revolution against the feudal order. Instead, the patricians acted to preserve their position against vigorous governments at the centre and a revolutionary tide among the poorer townsmen. However, we should not assume that any sort of new class war erupted in the towns of the Netherlands during the later sixteenth century. Throughout the late middle ages conflict had marked the relationship between the wealthy merchant class, who controlled the purchase and sale of manufactured goods, and the guildsmen who organised their production. The clash of interests between merchant-patricians and guildsmen expressed itself in the periodic uprisings and riots which mark the history of the towns of the Netherlands from the thirteenth century onwards. Lower down the social ladder, labourers and unskilled workers were also inclined to violence in times of shortage. Significantly, both 1566 and 1572 saw widespread hunger and unemployment. The popular movements which characterise these years undoubtedly owed much to the distress experienced by the lower orders.

* As in 1566, popular disaffection might lead to iconoclasm and anti-clerical excesses. Generally though, religious dissent was confined to a small group of persons. Throughout the sixteenth century never more than ten per cent of the Netherlands population was Protestant – and that figure applies also to the United Provinces of the 1590s. Of course the House of Orange and the estates of the rebel provinces were predominantly Calvinist in sympathy. They also had militant Calvinists among their supporters and it was the excesses of these which in part prompted the defection of the southern provinces in 1579. Nevertheless, the leading figures of the north belonged mainly to the 'libertinist' wing of the Calvinist movement. They were anxious to reduce the influence of the pastors and of the more radical religious elements. Thus, in the north during the 1580s, leadership was placed firmly in the hands of moderate politicians.

Although not primarily a religious struggle, the Revolt was affected by religion in two important ways. Firstly, because Philip II would not tolerate even a small number of heretics within the Netherlands, it was never possible to agree on the type of compromise solution that might have been possible if religion had not been a factor. As an English agent in the Netherlands remarked in 1574, 'The pride of the Spanish government and the cause of religion are the chief hindrance to a good accord.' Secondly, Philip's determination to wipe out heresy was opposed by a popular disgust of religious persecution. Historians have pointed out that we should detect in this resentment not a sympathy with heretical belief but, instead, a humanitarian concern for 'simple folk who have been misled'. In short, religion had its greatest impact in the opposing demands of Catholic orthodoxy and religious toleration rather than in terms of Catholic versus Calvinist. It is worth noting that, although Calvinism managed to establish itself as the exclusive religion of the United Provinces, freedom of conscience (as opposed to freedom of worship) was never denied there and no attempt was made to force everyone to share the same beliefs.

The preceding analysis is based on J. W. Smit's interpretation that the Revolt in the Netherlands was not inspired by one single grievance nor dominated by one single class. Instead the ambitions and interests of a number of different groups – grandees, lesser noblemen, patricians, guildsmen, poorer townsmen, Calvinists, and all those concerned for greater religious freedom – fed the Revolt, contributing to its complexity and character.

2 A War of Liberties

Despite what was argued in the previous section, it would be incorrect to portray the Revolt as merely a number of separate rebellions. One particular discontent was fundamental to all the different movements of rebellion. As a result of this 'common denominator' it is possible to speak of a single Revolt rather than just a spread of coinciding revolts.

The common denominator was a concern for liberties. The Netherlands of the sixteenth century was not a state in the modern sense of the word. It was a coalition of status-groups and privileged institutions. Provinces, nobility, towns and townsfolk: each enjoyed special rights which defined their relationship to the ruler and to one another. These liberties were sometimes written down in charters; more commonly they were just generally understood practices. Throughout the first half of the sixteenth century Charles V had been concerned not to override his subjects' liberties. Philip was not so careful. The inner council infringed the grandees' right to be heard by the Regent; the bishoprics plan challenged the nobility's traditional dominance of the church hierarchy; the persecution of heretics involved legal procedures which cut across the rights of local tribunals. Alva's Council of Troubles and collection of the Tenth Penny tax fuelled resentment. By the early 1570s every segment of society in the Netherlands felt that its special rights had in some way been infringed. All too often anti-Spanish feeling is singled out by historians as a major contributor to the Revolt. It is important to realise that resentment of Spain derived not from xenophobia (hatred of foreigners) but from the conviction that Philip II was not prepared to respect the liberties of his subjects.

The defence of liberties was an important component in the struggle of the 1570s and 1580s. All the major documents and treaties of the period stressed the need to preserve existing rights and to revive lost ones. The Pacification of Ghent spoke of the restoration of 'old privileges, customs and freedoms'; the Archduke Matthias was accepted as governor on condition that he maintained 'each and all of the privileges, rights, usages and customs of the country'; the signatories to the Utrecht Union similarly spoke of their readiness to uphold the special freedoms of the towns and provinces, as did the parties to the Peace of Arras; in 1581 Philip II was deposed by the States-General on account of his persistent disregard of his subjects' liberties. Even the revolutionary townsfolk defended the overthrow of municipal councils with the claim that they were acting to regain rights which the urban ruling class had set aside. However, when it came to defining precisely what their liberties were, all the interested parties found it hard either to enumerate or to substantiate their claims. Archives were ransacked and chests of documents opened in the hope that they would contain a record of lost liberties. Needless to say, none were found, as most liberties were the product either of unwritten customary practices or of fertile imaginations. Nevertheless, the widespread concern for the recovery of lost privileges lends support to the thesis that the Revolt was above all 'a war of liberties'.

Grandees, nobles and townsfolk rebelled against Spanish rule in order, therefore, to preserve the status quo and protect their old rights and privileges. Philip II was the revolutionary, not they, since he was the one most anxious to alter the traditional structure of government in the Netherlands. As one historian has put it, 'The rebellion against the Spanish authorities was a conservative revolution and could not have been otherwise – in those days it was not the rebels but the lawful governments who were the reformers and innovators.'

3 Reasons for the Success of the Revolt and for Spanish Failure

The interpretation offered so far goes a long way towards explaining the successful course taken by the Revolt. Because the Revolt was made up of a variety of overlapping movements, it possessed an endurance and capacity to withstand setbacks which a more narrowly based rebellion could not have enjoyed. The King of Spain was not just challenged by grandees, nobles, patricians, townsfolk, Calvinists and religious moderates operating in isolation, but by all of these joined together by a common concern for the restoration of liberties. For this reason, the defection or defeat of one group could not bring the Revolt to an end – as the desertion of the Catholic south in 1579 amply demonstrates.

There are of course many other reasons for Spanish failure. Military factors must be a major consideration. The tactics employed by the rebels, the quality and innovations of Maurice of Nassau and of his English allies can be identified as especially important. Alva's strategy, the mutinies of the Spanish army and its diversion, even in victory, to other theatres of war also contributed. Additionally, the terrain of the Netherlands hampered the Spanish programme of reconquest. The many bogs and fortified towns, all of which required lengthy sieges, prevented the Spaniards from taking full advantage of their numerical superiority. However, the view proposed over half a century ago by Pieter Geyl (see Further Reading, page 112) that the great rivers – the Waal, Maas and Lek – provided an impregnable barrier behind which the rebels could shelter, has been exposed as untenable. The rivers could be crossed by the Spanish armies with relative ease, as happened in 1605, and Maurice constructed his line of fortifications on the assumption that the river-line might be breached. In any case, most of the fighting took place south of the great rivers and the eventual boundary between the United Provinces and the Spanish provinces did not follow any obvious geographical feature.

Behind the military explanations lie the economic ones. The boom in the United Provinces may be contrasted with Spain's perennial shortage of cash and with the economic decay of the southern provinces. In short, Spain did not have the resources to defeat the rebels. However, to say that Philip lacked the means can only be a partial explanation for Spanish failure. Spain far outstripped every other European state in the extent of her empire, the scale of her revenues and the size of her armies. Of all the monarchs of Christendom, Philip might have been expected to encompass the defeat of a few rebellious provinces. For the King of Spain, though, the Netherlands ranked as only one concern of many. The defence of the Mediterranean, the preservation of the Catholic religion in strife-torn France, and measures of dynastic aggrandisement such as the annexation of Portugal: these were obligations which Philip also felt bound to discharge. Therefore, he frequently had to divide his resources to meet his many commitments.

If we analyse the Revolt from the point of view of Spain, a fresh appreciation of the reasons for Philip's ultimate failure in the Netherlands may be gained. During the early 1560s, Philip's main interest was the Mediterranean. In order to counter the Turkish threat, all the resources of Spain had to be deployed there. Hence Philip let the grandees' revolt against Granvelle proceed largely unchecked. In 1566 the Sultan Suleiman the Magnificent died and the Turkish Empire dissolved into civil war. Alva could now be despatched. By 1570, though, the Turks were returning to strength and Spanish funds which had previously fed the Netherlands were diverted once more to the Mediterranean. Alva was left with insufficient receipts from Spain – hence his ruthless attempt to collect the Tenth Penny which in turn contributed to a fresh uprising in the Netherlands. Between 1572 and 1576 Spain was fighting on two fronts. Unable to bear the strain, the treasury bankrupted. Shortly afterwards, Don John recognised the Pacification of Ghent and with Philip's permission withdrew all Spanish forces from the Netherlands.

No sooner had peace in the Netherlands been secured than Philip managed to conclude a truce with the Sultan (1577). The King was, therefore, able to renew the war, and under Don John and then Parma the reconquest proceeded. But no sooner were resources earmarked for the Netherlands than a new crisis intervened. With the death of the heirless King Sebastian of Portugal in 1578, Philip began his struggle for the Portuguese crown. To meet the needs of the war in Portugal, Parma's army was reduced in size, although this in itself did not rob him of victory. As one historian has remarked, it is interesting to speculate what Parma might have achieved had he been given full access to Spanish troops and money. Even after the annexation of Portugal in 1582, Spanish troops and money continued to be denied the generals in the Netherlands. The war with England and then with France took up the lion's share of Spanish money in the late 1580s and 1590s. Bankruptcy, mutiny and defeat were the result of these additional burdens.

In order to comprehend the reasons for Spanish defeat in the conflict of 1566–1609 we need to extend our enquiry beyond the Netherlands. The rebels were fighting an empire. In that empire's extended commitments and many concerns may be found an important explanation for its eventual defeat in the north-western corner of Europe.

Making Notes on *'The Revolt Analysed'*

This chapter is less concerned with 'facts' than with presenting ideas and possible interpretations. The first two sections provide new ways of viewing the Revolt and these should give you a method of analysis which can be used to answer a variety of different questions. The third section fulfils a twofold function. Firstly it recapitulates several of the points made at greater lengths earlier on in the text. Secondly, it attempts to put the revolt in its European and Spanish context, which in turn produces additional reasons for the Revolt's success.

The following headings and questions should help you make suitable notes:

1.   How many revolts?
1.1. Historians' opinions
1.2. The Smit thesis. What is the major point of the Smit thesis?
1.3. Religion. What were the two important effects religion had on the course of the Revolt?
2.   A war of liberties. What is meant by liberties'?
3.   Reasons for the success of the Revolt and for Spanish failure. What

was the single most important reason for Spain's failure to crush the rebels?

Answering essay-questions on The Revolt 1566–1609

The vast majority of essay-questions on the Revolt at A-level will require you to take an overview of the whole period from 1566 to 1609. It is a common fault among students to imagine that in some way the Revolt petered out in the 1570s and that the events of the following years can be ignored even when the question makes the time-span quite clear:

> 'Why were the Dutch able to defy Spain so successfully between 1568 and 1609?'

> ' "It was less any particular ability on the part of the Dutch than the foolishness of Philip II himself which decided the outcome of the Dutch Revolt". Discuss.'

The first of these questions can be planned with a 'because scheme'. The problem is that you will end up with a list of about a dozen or more points, so that your essay could as a consequence read too much like a list. In order to avoid this, divide the essay in two, explaining firstly Dutch strengths and then Spanish weaknesses. For the conclusion summarise your main points and explain briefly which in your opinion contributed the most to Dutch success.

The second question is of the 'quote-and-discuss' variety. It is a mistake to think that this type of question allows you more scope than a question beginning with a 'why', and that you can therefore ramble around the Revolt until 45 minutes have elapsed. Establish firstly what the abilities of the Dutch were, then where Philip II may have been guilty of foolishness. Try to end with a conclusion that establishes firmly which of the two possibilities carries the greater conviction.

It was common last century for Dutch historians to explain the Revolt as a religious uprising. More recent historians usually push religion on to the sidelines. The reasons for this are summarised by J. W. Smit in his criticism of one nineteenth-century Dutch Calvinist historian, Groen van Prinsterer, 'There are many facts to contradict his conception, such as the great number of Catholics and 'politiques' taking part in the opposition in the 1560s, in the so-called revolution of the people in the provinces of Holland and Zealand in 1572, and also in the new uprising in 1576 in the provinces which had remained quiet after the defeat of the revolution in 1566. There is also, for example, the fact that the act by which the rest of the rebellious provinces abjured King Philip in 1581 alleged no religious reason in justification.'

Despite this historiographical change, A-level questions often raise the problem of religion:

'To what extent was the Dutch Revolt a war of religion?'

'What was the role of religion in the Revolt of the Netherlands 1566–1609?'

As far as the first question is concerned you will probably find it easier to argue that the Revolt was not a war of religion. In framing your essay, bear in mind and elaborate the objections raised by Smit; consider also the small number of Protestants in the Netherlands during the sixteenth century. Nevertheless the easier approach may not necessarily yield the right answer. Also, historians' opinions change and you should not presume that today's explanation will hold in the future. As an alternative, therefore, you may choose to argue that the Revolt was above all a religious uprising. If so, then you may like to concentrate your analysis on the Iconoclast Fury, on the role of the Calvinist Sea Beggars, and on the religious disagreements of 1576–79. Also, look back in your notes under heading 1.3. of this chapter for an additional and more sophisticated way of tackling this type of question.

CHAPTER 6

The United Provinces 1609–1650

1 Remonstrants and Contra-Remonstrants

In 1673 a former English ambassador to The Hague made the following comments on the government and political organisation of the United Provinces:

1   It cannot be properly styled a commonwealth, but is rather a
    confederacy of seven sovereign provinces united together for their
    common and mutual defence . . . But to discover the nature of
    their government from the first springs and motions, it must be
5   taken yet into smaller pieces, by which it will appear that each of
    these provinces is likewise composed of many little states or cities,
    which have several marks of sovereign power within themselves,
    and are not subject to the sovereignty of their province . . . For as
    the States-General cannot make war or peace, or any new alliance,
10 or levies of money without the consent of every province, so cannot
    the provincial estates conclude any of those points without the
    consent of each of the cities, that by their constitution has a voice in
    that assembly.

Although the author of this passage was writing much later than the events of this chapter, his account applies equally well to our period. The United Provinces did not have – and never would have – a strong central government. Instead, power was decentralised and shared among local instruments: town councils and provincial estates. The States-General, although entrusted with the collective sovereignty of the country, was really just the forum in which the interests of the seven provinces were presented by their advocates. The provincial estates, which drew up the advocates' instructions, similarly consisted of delegates who had to refer back to their appointing bodies for advice and directions. The only 'national institution' in the United Provinces was the House of Orange which provided the *stadholders* in all seven provinces. But however much the *stadholders* might exceed their powers later on, they were technically only the servants of the provincial estates which had appointed them and they were not free to do as they chose in public affairs.

   * During the war years, Oldenbarnevelt had managed to prevent the decentralised structure of government in the United Provinces from degenerating into a shambles of local rivalries. The province of Holland, of which he was the advocate, contributed two-thirds of the United Provinces' military budget and much of the manpower of the army besides. By threatening to withhold resources Oldenbarnevelt could impose his own and Holland's will on the deputies and estates of the other six provinces.

Once peace was made with Spain, the need to follow Holland's lead lessened and complaints began to be voiced against Holland's continued political dominance. Criticism swiftly focused on Oldenbarnevelt. The estates of the other coastal provinces, led by Zealand, resented Oldenbarnevelt's continual backing of Holland's commercial interests which they saw as rivalling their own. For their part, the inland provinces considered Oldenbarnevelt to be the representative of trade and industry whereas their own economies were largely based on agriculture. Amsterdam, although a town in Holland, joined the side of the other six provinces, claiming that during the negotiations for the 1609 truce Oldenbarnevelt had at Spain's request deliberately sabotaged its scheme for a West Indies Company.

* It was religion which fuelled these resentments and eventually brought down Oldenbarnevelt. The majority of the urban ruling class – the patricians who dominated the provincial estates and the States-General – belonged to the latitudinarian or libertinist wing of Dutch Calvinism. They wanted a broadly tolerant church which was attractive to the majority of Dutch Christians, for Calvinists were still a minority in the United Provinces. In addition, they were anxious to maintain their control over the church, appointing ministers as they chose and not having the clergy interfere in the business of government. In other words, they subscribed to erastianism, which is the view that the church should be subordinate to the state. Most of the clergy held a quite different opinion. They believed in doctrinal correctness even if this made Calvinism severe and forbidding. Instead of erastianism, they wanted theocracy. They argued that the clergy's role was to create the Kingdom of God on earth and that the true function of government was to help them achieve this end in accordance with their own recommendations.

Until the second decade of the seventeenth century there seemed little chance that the ideas of the Calvinist clergy would prevail. The town councils vigorously opposed the construction of a Calvinist theocracy and they used their right to dismiss ministers in such a way as to curb the more extreme preachers. Oldenbarnevelt and the States-General supported the townsmen even to the extent of rewriting the constitution of the Calvinist church in the Netherlands. However, during the early years of the seventeenth century, doctrinal questions assumed a new importance and fast became caught up with the movement of opposition to Oldenbarnevelt and the estates of Holland. As a consequence the Calvinist clergy found unexpected allies.

In 1602 a theologian called Arminius was appointed a professor at Leiden University in Holland. Arminius' teachings contradicted a basic element of Calvinist theology. John Calvin had argued that since God is all-powerful and all-knowing, he must have decided in the first place who was to be saved and who to be damned. This theory of predestination was repellant to Arminius. He argued that Christ had died to save all and not just a few 'elect' chosen by Him in advance. Instead, Arminius said, individuals by their own free will chose or rejected the path to salvation.

Arminius never claimed that the Calvinist creed was incorrect in any of its other teachings and until his death in 1609 he remained a member of the Reformed Church. However, by questioning the doctrine of predestination, he struck at a main element of Calvinist belief. In addition, Arminius' doctrine of freewill seemed suspiciously similar to Catholic teachings, to which the Calvinist clergy in the Netherlands were unalterably opposed. Arminius and the band of disciples he gathered round him were therefore fiercely criticised for their views.

The small but growing number of Arminian Calvinists first attempted to rebut criticism in pamphlets and in formal debates. This only inflamed passions. Local synods pressed for the dismissal of Arminian ministers and boycotts of their churches were arranged. The strict Calvinists coupled their resistance to the new teaching with the demand that a national synod of the Dutch Calvinist Church he called to discuss Arminius' theories. They knew that they would hold the majority in the synod and could use this forum to condemn Arminianism as heresy.

* As the Arminians were unable to gather support in the church hierarchy, they turned elsewhere. In Holland, where the most bitter contest between Arminians and strict Calvinists was being fought out, they applied to the provincial estates for help. In 1610 the Arminian clergy presented to the Holland estates a written *Remonstrance*. In this document they outlined their teachings, asked for protection and called on the estates to revise the current definition of the Calvinist faith to make it fit in better with their beliefs.

Led by Oldenbarnevelt (who probably had a hand in framing the *Remonstrance*), the estates of Holland accepted the petition and over the next few years intervened in church affairs to defend the Remonstrants. The estates pronounced that both the Arminian and the strict Calvinist doctrines of salvation were equally acceptable beliefs. Churchmen opposed to Arminian ideas drew up in reply their own statement of belief known as the *Contra-Remonstrance*. The Contra-Remonstrants presented the case for maintaining predestination as the exclusive doctrine of salvation. They firmly rejected the estates' erastian intervention in a theological dispute and repeated that doctrine could only be changed by a national synod. Because the Contra-Remonstrant clergy refused to accept the verdict of the estates that they should tolerate Arminian opinions, many of their number were expelled from churches in Holland. But they continued to hold services in fields, as a consequence of which they earned the name of 'mud-beggars'.

Between 1610 and 1618 the quarrel between the Remonstrants and the Contra-Remonstrants grew furiously. But Oldenbarnevelt and the estates of Holland continued to embrace the cause of toleration and did their best to ensure that Arminian views could still be presented in the churches of Holland. However, in the case of Oldenbarnevelt we should not imagine that his support for the Remonstrants derived from deep religious convictions. In 1617 Oldenbarnevelt discussed his motives with Dudley Carleton, the English ambassador, who made the following notes of their conversation:

1 He [Oldenbarnevelt] said that the strongest, soundest and richest part of the country were papists, another great part were Lutherans, some were [atheists] and very many here in Holland Anabaptists . . . The Protestant part was not the third of the inhabitants
5 and was divided betwixt those he termed puritans and double-puritans (for such he said we held them in England) . . . Above all things he wished to avoid the division or separation of churches which if there was no remedy must be yielded unto. He foresaw schism and, from schism, faction and confusion. The professed
10 religion in these provinces, he said, was without order or rule or any form of government . . . Since the framing of the truce he with others had endeavoured to bring the church here under the like government as was exercised in England, France, Geneva, Germany and other reformed churches which could not be done but by
15 giving the like authority to the States-General and to the particular towns, as was acknowledged in other places of the same profession in religion . . . In the end of our discourse he professed his own opinion was clear in the point of predestination wherein he was satisfied in his youth at Heidelberg and therefore he was contrary in
20 judgment touching this particular to Arminius, but seeing that the government of the state [i.e. the Holland estates] had judged both opinions to be tolerated he could not but stand for the maintenance of their authority.

In other words, Oldenbarnevelt was personally unconvinced by Arminius' teachings, having been won over to the doctrine of predestination while a student at Heidelberg University. His support for the Remonstrants was based on his realisation that the United Provinces contained people of many different creeds. Catholics were still the largest denomination but there were Lutherans, Anabaptists and various shades of Calvinist there as well. To allow one sect to dominate exclusively the affairs of church and state would upset the fragile unity of the new republic. Far better a church which tolerated different theological views and which was subject to orderly control by the States-General.

Oldenbarnevelt's stance in the religious controversy was therefore largely determined by political considerations. For reasons having even less to do with religion, others lined up behind the Contra-Remonstrants. The town council of Amsterdam refused to dismiss its Contra-Remonstrant clergy, hoping thereby to embarrass Oldenbarnevelt and oblige him to reconsider the proposal for a Dutch West Indies Company. The estates of Zealand, Friesland, Groningen and Gelderland supported the Contra-Remonstrant demand for a national synod, deliberately pitting themselves against Holland. For reasons that are obscure, but which may be related to a personal estrangement between Oldenbarnevelt and himself, the *stadholder* Maurice also drifted towards the Contra-Remonstrant side.

* Emboldened by the extent of their support, the Contra-Remonstrants began a vigorous offensive and started to reoccupy the churches from which they had been ejected. Early in 1617 Contra-Remonstrant mud-beggars entered The Hague and began holding services within earshot of Oldenbarnevelt's home. The outraged Advocate demanded that Maurice enter the town with troops and expel the preachers. As *stadholder* of Holland, Maurice was responsible for maintaining order and for performing such tasks as the estates commanded. Maurice, however, refused the order. As he admitted, he did not know whether predestination was blue or green and the debates of theologians were of no interest to him. But he was not prepared to sacrifice his reputation for a cause which had created such ill-feeling. Oldenbarnevelt responded to Maurice's defiance by having the estates of Holland pass the 'sharp resolution' in August 1617. Town councils in Holland were told to recruit their own troops with which to expel Contra-Remonstrant ministers, and army units were required to offer assistance.

The 'sharp resolution' was both a challenge to Maurice's authority as *stadholder* and the sign that religious disagreement was about to lead to armed confrontation. Maurice acted cautiously but effectively. Having first ensured his support in the estates of the other six provinces, Maurice had the States-General meet and declare the 'sharp resolution' invalid. Then in August 1618, with the estates of Holland still refusing to rescind the resolution, he invaded Holland, installed his own men in the town councils and arrested Oldenbarnevelt and the Holland estates. After a show trial, the Advocate was beheaded in May 1619 on the charge of treason. (This penalty seems unjustifiably severe. Probably though, the sentence was passed with the aim of frightening Oldenbarnevelt into making a public confession, after which he would have been pardoned. Since Oldenbarnevelt refused to admit any guilt, the sentence had to stand.)

In the struggle between Remonstrants and Contra-Remonstrants the loser is obvious: Oldenbarnevelt. It is less easy to decide the victor. Late in 1618 a national synod met at Dordt. The synod affirmed the traditional doctrine of predestination, banned Arminian teachings and drove Remonstrant ministers into exile. It also listed a whole series of prohibitions against such things as carnivals, strolling players and drinking clubs, which were considered 'to entice the people away from holiness'. Some historians have argued that the 'sober modesty' of Dutch seventeenth-century life was the direct consequence of these enactments. However, the synod won no concessions in respect of church-state relations. Ministers continued to be appointed and dismissed by town councils and they were not given any share in political decision making. The most they could secure was a purge of Remonstrant and Catholic town officials – and many of these were back in place by the late 1620s. Nor was the power of Holland curtailed. Since Holland continued paying the lion's share of the United Provinces' overall budget, it was inevitable – especially after the war with Spain was renewed in 1621 – that its counsels should prevail in meetings of the States-General. By the 1630s the new Advocate of Holland, or as he was now known Grand Pensionary, wielded as much influence in the States-General as his predecessor, Oldenbarnevelt. Perhaps the greatest beneficiary of the Remonstrant crisis was the House of Orange. Once again, but now in peacetime and in a purely domestic crisis, the *stadholder* had intervened decisively to end discord. The House of Orange stood thus confirmed as the embodiment of the United Provinces and the main defence against political fragmentation.

2 The War with Spain 1621–48

The 'Twelve-Years Truce' agreed at Antwerp in 1609 ushered in a period of cold war between the United Provinces and Spain. Each side now tried to outmanoeuvre the other and to seize some advantage in readiness for 1621 when hostilities were due to recommence. In 1609–14 (over the Jülich-Cleves succession crisis) and in 1619–20 (in the Bohemian War) the truce almost broke down. On both these occasions Spain and the United Provinces narrowly avoided being drawn into a general European conflict on opposing sides. But, as it turned out, only on the high seas was blood shed when continued Dutch penetration of Spanish markets provoked arrests and retaliation.

The 1609 truce had allowed for its renewal on expiry. As the twelve years neared their conclusion, though, neither side pressed for a new treaty. The main source of influence in the Spanish court had passed in 1618 to the 'hawks' led at first by the Duke of Zuñiga and then, after 1622, by the Count-Duke of Olivares. Zuñiga convinced King Philip III that the terms of the 1609 truce were disadvantageous both to Spain's interests and to her reputation, and that more favourable conditions should be extracted from the Dutch, by force if need be. The conditions Zuñiga had in mind and which were communicated to the Dutch were freedom of worship for Dutch Catholics, the reopening of the Scheldt estuary – and thus the revival of Antwerp's commerce – and a Dutch withdrawal from Spanish possessions in the Indies. The death of Philip III in 1621 and the accession of his son, Philip IV, did not change Spanish policy towards the United Provinces.

In the United Provinces the execution of Oldenbarnevelt had eliminated the architect of the 1609 truce and put power in the hands of a war party led by Amsterdam. Amsterdam's leading citizens wanted to extend their town's commercial strength abroad at Spain's expense, mainly by establishing a West Indies Company to encroach on the trade of the New World. Once the Spanish terms for a renewal of the truce were known, commercial considerations brought Holland and the other coastal provinces over to Amsterdam's side.

* The Dutch-Spanish war of 1621–48 was therefore quite different from the struggle between 1572 and 1609. In the earlier conflict the Spaniards and the rebels both had as their aim the complete removal of their opponents from the territory of the Netherlands. The new war was fought with more limited objectives in mind. The Spanish were primarily interested in obtaining a better settlement; the Dutch with preventing this and with winning new commercial opportunities.

The land war which followed the expiry of the truce in 1621 consisted almost entirely of sieges. Only on one occasion, in 1638 at Kallo, did a full set-piece battle take place. For the rest the war was a matter of blockades, enlivened only by the occasional sally through the strong lines of fortifications both sides erected for their defence. The commander of the Spanish forces, Ambrosio Spinola, took Jülich in 1622 and, three years later, Breda. This was, however, the sum total of his successes. Neither he nor his successor, the Cardinal-Infant Ferdinand, brother of Philip IV, were able to extend Spanish control into the interior of the United Provinces. On the Dutch side, Maurice of Nassau took Cleves in 1625. Following his death that year, command of the Dutch armies together with all the offices of *stadholder* which he had held, were assumed by his younger brother, Frederick Henry. In 1629 Frederick Henry conquered s'Hertogenbosch; three years later he seized Maastricht and in 1637 he recaptured Breda. But his attempts to carry the war deep into the southern provinces and to take Antwerp proved unsuccessful.

The war at sea proved similarly inconclusive. In 1621 the Amsterdammers won the States-General's permission to set up a West Indies Company. In 1627 ships of the Company captured 55 Spanish vessels in the Caribbean and, a year later, at the Battle of Matanzas Bay, fought off the Cuban coast, the entire Spanish silver fleet fell into Dutch hands. But these successes were exceptional and in all other years the Company fared badly. By the 1640s Amsterdam and the now nearly bankrupt Company had become, ironically, strong advocates of peace.

Affairs in the East Indies proved less disastrous. Although the Dutch East India Company conquered neither Manila nor Macao, two of its main objectives, it still managed to capture a good part of Spanish trade in this region. From the island of Taiwan the Dutch began their penetration of Chinese commerce and from Sri Lanka and Malacca, which they captured in 1641, extended their economic involvement on the Indian and Malayan coast.

A number of explanations may be given for the largely inconclusive and static nature of the Spanish-Dutch war of 1621–48. Firstly, neither side was committed to an extensive programme of conquest. Instead, both the Spanish and the Dutch viewed the war as an exercise in 'diplomacy by other means'. Thus, throughout the conflict, peace conferences regularly met as each side tried to use its latest victory as a bargaining counter in negotiations. Secondly, as far as the land war was concerned, the nature of the fighting with its procession of sieges precluded swift victories. As Spinola lamented, 'In order to capture a rebel town, an entire summer and army may be consumed without any certain success'.

In addition, both Spain and the United Provinces had insufficient resources for prolonged and vigorous campaigning. During the 1620s taxes in the United Provinces rose by almost 50 per cent and as a consequence there were outbreaks of unrest in several towns. By the 1630s the estates of Holland were showing a marked reluctance to finance any campaigns which were not strictly defensive. Since Holland provided two-thirds of the war budget, this imposed a severe constraint on the Dutch command. There is also some evidence to suggest that the United Provinces lacked the necessary manpower to sustain both the war and a commercial economy. In 1635 the English ambassador to The Hague reported home to his superior that he did not believe the Dutch 'can easily or suddenly find sufficient plenty of mariners and seamen to drive their trade and commerce by sea and uphold their men-of-war and navigation generally with honour and advantage.' The ambassador pointed out that a fifth of the manpower of the Dutch fleet consisted already of Englishmen and Scots.

Between 1621 and 1648 Spain was not only engaged in fighting the Dutch but also in propping up the Habsburg cause in the general European conflict known as 'The Thirty Years War'. For this reason Spain was unable to make a wholehearted commitment to the Dutch war. In 1629 Spanish forces were diverted from north-west Europe to Italy where they took part in the War of the Mantuan Succession. Five years later the Cardinal-Infant Ferdinand, commander of the Spanish forces in the Netherlands, was instructed to help the Emperor's troops fight the Swedes in southern Germany. In 1635 France entered the Thirty Years War against Spain and the Habsburgs and, by its intervention, compelled the deployment of Spanish units along the southern frontier of the Netherlands. At the same time, the Dutch exploited the wider European war to win military aid from England, Denmark, France and Sweden.

* The Spanish government in Madrid was only too well aware of the limitations it faced in fighting the Dutch. For this reason the decision was made at an early stage in the conflict to practise an entirely new form of warfare. This development has only recently attracted the notice of historians. However, it is clear that the 'new warfare' came close to defeating the Dutch and forcing their agreement to disadvantageous peace terms.

Even in the last years of the sixteenth century, Spanish commanders in the Netherlands were viewing with interest the possibility of an economic blockade of the United Provinces. The idea was revived in the early 1620s. As one adviser to Philip IV noted, 'Since the Dutch derive all their gains from trade . . . should they lose this commerce they shall be less powerful enemies and we can expect a good settlement favourable to Spain.' During the 1620s, therefore, Spain audaciously chose to challenge the Dutch where they were strongest – on the sea – and a naval blockade of the United Provinces started. The first stage in the economic war was the exclusion of Dutch vessels from Spanish ports. To ensure that the Dutch did not attempt to use neutrals to get round the restrictions on their trade, the Northern Board of Admiralty (*almirantazgo*) was established in 1624 to inquire into the origins of cargoes and issue licenses. Next, an *armada* of thirty galleons was constructed to patrol the English Channel and the North Sea and to harrass Dutch shipping. Full encouragement and support at sea was also given to privateers who, operating mainly from Dunkirk, could devastate the Dutch herring fleets. The success achieved by the *armada* and the privateers was staggering. Between 1629 and 1638 almost 2000 Dutch ships were captured and about a thousand sunk. As a result, marine insurance and freight charges soared making Dutch commerce increasingly unprofitable. Trade routes were lost to English and French merchants and the Dutch textile industry went into slump.

Had the Spanish government been able to maintain an effective blockade it seems probable that the Dutch economy would have been driven into bankruptcy. However, by the 1630s the Dutch fleet was able to turn the tables by establishing its own blockade of the pirates' nest at Dunkirk. In 1639 an armada despatched by Philip IV to restore Spanish naval supremacy in Flemish waters was soundly defeated by the Dutch Admiral Tromp in the Battle of the Downs.

Unfortunately for Spain, the blockade proved highly damaging to the Spanish as well as the Dutch economy, since Spain depended on Dutch shipping both for imports and for exports. As one critic later wrote, 'The *almirantazgo* closed the door to all commerce . . . such that within a short time Spain was without trade, ships or foodstuffs, customs revenue fell and the country's produce had no means of exit.' The same circumstance applied to the Spanish Netherlands, where as early as 1629 overland trade with the north had to be allowed so as to save Flemish industry from decay and the Spanish garrisons from starvation. In 1644 Philip IV gave Dutch vessels permission to enter ports in southern Spain to provide grain; three years later the economic blockade was lifted entirely.

* Formal negotiations for peace were commenced in 1646 at Münster. The Spanish government, which was now preoccupied with the war with France and had already suffered the secession of Portugal and Catalonia, was anxious to rid itself of its entanglement with the Dutch. The towns and estates of the United Provinces were for the most part

convinced that peace would provide better commercial prospects than war had done. Also, they had news of secret negotiations between Spain and France which would allow the southern provinces to be absorbed into France in exchange for French help in restoring Spanish rule in Catalonia. The Dutch judged that a weak and chastened Spanish government in the southern provinces would be preferable to an expansionist French one. The death of the *stadholder* Frederick Henry in 1647 removed the main opponent to the peace party. Frederick Henry's son and successor, William II, lacked the resolve and experience to carry on the now unpopular war.

Although it took time to win all the political forces in the United Provinces round to giving their consent to the Peace of Münster (1648), the treaty was distinctly to the advantage of the Dutch. Philip IV agreed that all parts of the Spanish provinces conquered by the Dutch armies would be recognised as part of the Republic. Dutch possessions in the West and East Indies would similarly be respected. Philip also promised that Dutch vessels would not be impeded in Spanish ports and that the Scheldt would remain closed so preventing a revival of Antwerp's commerce.

The most important clause of the treaty was that in which Spain formally recognised the independence of the seven northern provinces of the Netherlands and renounced all rights of sovereignty over these. With a thrilling sense of occasion the publication of the treaty was delayed in the United Provinces until 5 April 1648. The reason was explained by the Portuguese ambassador to The Hague who wrote in a despatch, 'The peace was proclaimed here by reading the articles of the Treaty in the Supreme Court of Justice at ten o'clock on the morning of the fifth of this month, that day and hour being chosen because on that day and at that hour eighty years ago the Counts of Egmont and Hornes had been executed by the Duke of Alva in Brussels; and the estates wanted their freedom to begin at the same day and time as those two gentlemen had died in defence thereof.'

3 Economy and Society

The Dutch economy in the seventeenth century rested on fishing, on long-distance trade and on industry. As in the previous conflict with Spain, the Republic's economic capacity sustained the war and preserved the independence of the new state during the war of 1621–48. Realising this, the Spanish government tried by its blockading strategy to undermine the foundation of the Republic's prosperity, reckoning that the Dutch would then be unable to maintain their war effort. Spain's failure to bankrupt the United Provinces allowed not only the economic survival and eventual victory of the Republic but also the continued development there of an essentially middle-class state.

The Dutch herring fleet, which operated mainly from Rotterdam and

Enkhuizen, consisted of about two thousand 'busses', specially designed boats capable of pulling large trawls and of curing fish on deck. The busses dominated the 'Grand Fishery' of the North Sea and the fields of cod off Iceland. It is estimated that about a third of the Dutch population were in some way engaged in or dependent on fishing, and that the annual herring catch amounted in value to about two million pounds sterling: the equivalent of Britain's own yearly cloth exports. Rightly did one contemporary remark that the Grand Fishery was 'the chiefest trade and principal gold mine' of the United Provinces. In addition to the herring industry, an Arctic whaling fleet was built up in Amsterdam to supply the 'train oil' needed for soap and for fuelling lamps. A Dutch whaling-station operated ten degrees north of the Arctic circle at Spitzbergen.

Amsterdam led the way in Dutch international trade and in the commerce of north-western Europe generally. In this respect Amsterdam took over the role previously played by Antwerp, which had been under almost continual blockade since the 1580s. The Amsterdammers, and Dutch merchants as a whole, were primarily engaged in transporting commodities for resale, not in supplying a domestic market. As late as 1728 Daniel Defoe could still describe the Dutch as 'the carriers of the world, the middle persons in trade, the factors and brokers of Europe . . . They buy to sell again, take in to send out, and the greatest part of this vast commerce consists of being supplied from all parts of the world that they may supply all the world again.'

The main area of Dutch mercantile activity was the Baltic Sea where grain was purchased in exchange for wine, fish and textiles. The grain was then shipped via Holland, where some was diverted for home consumption, on to Spain, France and the Mediterranean. By the 1620s two-thirds of all shipping entering the Baltic through the Danish Sound consisted of Dutch vessels, while of the entire Dutch merchant fleet well over a third was engaged in Baltic commerce. Additionally, the Dutch dealt in Swedish and Austrian metals and in English and German textiles. They even ferried coal from Newcastle to London. All in all, the number of Dutch ships was by 1650 greater than those of the rest of Europe put together.

Less significant for Dutch prosperity – it accounted for only seven per cent of total shipping and profits were seldom spectacular – was the Indies trade. During the seventeenth century the East India Company gradually extended the number of its trading posts, called 'factories', in the western Pacific and Indian Ocean. By 1650 the Company had stations in the Moluccas, Java, Malaya, India, Ceylon (Sri Lanka) and Taiwan. These factories provided spices, tea and silk which were transported back to Holland for sale and re-export. After 1639 The East India Company also enjoyed a monopoly of Japanese commerce from which was obtained silver, gold and copper. The West Indies Company, after an unsuccessful attempt to establish trading posts in north-east Brazil

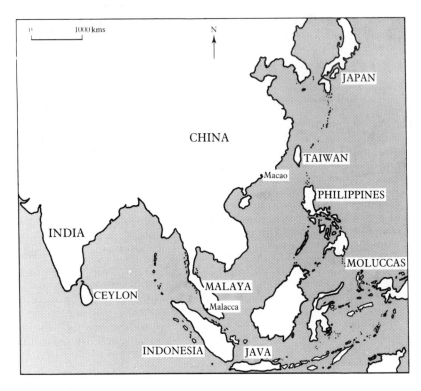

Trading posts of the East India Company, 1650

and in Angola, had turned its attention by the middle of the century to the gold mines of the Guinea coast and the slave trade with Spanish America. Only in two places did the Dutch found colonies: on Manhattan Island in 1624 and on the Cape of Good Hope in 1652. The first of these was taken by the English in the 1660s and its name was changed from New Amsterdam to New York. The colony on the Cape only really developed in the eighteenth century, due to the endeavours of the Dutch agricultural settlers. For the most part, the Dutch were content to set up fortified factories and to win over the local potentates.

    * Dutch commerce, both in Europe and elsewhere, was sustained by a formidable array of financial mechanisms which ensured that business confidence was maintained and that private capital was harnessed for trading purposes. Marine insurance began in the 1590s and was soon put under the regulatory supervision of a Chamber of Assurance. In the 1660s even the bullion of Spanish treasure galleons was insured in Amsterdam. By 1608 Amsterdam had its own stockmarket and within the space of a few years gained a grain market, exchange bank and

lending bank. Joint-stock ventures, which allowed small investors to become partners in commercial enterprises, flourished; the willing subscriber could as easily buy a share in a fishing buss as purchase East India Company stock.

Industry provided alternative opportunities for investment, which in turn stimulated growth. In Leiden, Amsterdam, and Haarlem, cloth was manufactured and 'finished' by dyeing, bleaching and dressing, ready for export. In shipbuilding the Dutch were at the forefront of technical advance. With their cranes, sawmills and other labour-saving devices, they could undercut the price of their English competitors by over a third. Along with ship construction went a range of ancillary industries: rope yards, chandling and naval munitions.

Agriculture benefited from continued investment in land reclamation schemes and in the construction of new dykes. The purchase of land in the countryside by wealthy townsmen also injected both cash and entrepreneurial direction into Dutch farming. Stock breeding, the abolition of fallow by crop rotation, and the development of industrial crops, such as flax and hemp, followed. However, this was a phenomenon confined largely to Holland and the coastal provinces. In Gelderland and Overijssel traditional farming methods survived along with an impoverished feudal class of petty nobility.

Although the agricultural economy was in places advanced, the wealth of the United Provinces rested overwhelmingly on trade and industry. As a consequence, the population of the United Provinces tended to concentrate in the towns, where employment could be more readily found. Already by the 1620s, 56 per cent of the inhabitants of Holland were urban dwellers, with almost a sixth of the population crammed into Amsterdam. By the 1650s it may be reckoned that well over a half of the entire Dutch population were townsfolk.

* Elsewhere in Europe, wherever an agricultural economy prevailed and the population lived mainly on the land, political power rested in the hands of the landowning class, which was still largely synomymous with the nobility. By contrast, in the United Provinces the combination of a largely town-based population with a powerful trading and industrial economy resulted in political leadership being assumed by the urban élites. In the provincial estates of Holland, the vote of the towns outnumbered that of the nobility by eighteen to one. In Zealand, Utrecht, Friesland and Groningen the urban interest similarly predominated. Only in the largely rural and backward provinces of Overijssel and Gelderland were the nobles able to retain their ascendancy in the provincial estates.

The urban élites, which dominated all the other provincial estates and therefore the States-General, consisted of a small group of patricians. They were appointed to civic office by cooption rather than by popular election and for this reason they were able as a class to preserve their political leadership. Until about 1650 these patrician oligarchies consisted mainly of very wealthy businessmen who had made their fortunes in the Baltic trade, the North Sea fisheries, in shipping and industry. The families of the patricians often intermarried and son succeeded father on the town councils. However, the urban patriciate was not at all a closed group. The newly rich were admitted to its ranks while patrician families which suffered impoverishment soon found themselves excluded from influence. Only in the second half of the seventeenth century did the ruling groups in the towns pass restrictions to prevent the influx of new blood to their ranks and, instead of trade, put their energies into finance, property ownership for rent, and acquiring stately manor houses in the countryside. In this way the patricians of the seventeenth-century 'Golden Age' were superseded by the so-called 'regents' of the eighteenth-century 'Periwig period'.

Below the urban patriciate were the less successful merchants and the skilled craftsmen. Most foreign accounts commented on the sobriety and thrift of these groups which gave them the savings with which to invest in business ventures. The smaller merchants and traders were generally 'content to have little share in government, desiring only security in what they possess'. However, they were eager to make a good match for their children and lift them into the ranks of the patrician class. The craftsmen for their part maintained the guild system throughout the seventeenth century thus preventing newcomers and outsiders from setting up in competition.

Possibly as much as 40 per cent of the urban population consisted of the *grauw* or 'rabble', who were the casual labourers and lowest class of town dweller. The *grauw* tended to live in cellars and back-premises whence they issued daily in their search for employment. In times of hardship the *grauw* were ready to take to the streets and to organise violent strikes for better pay or to riot for work. To control 'the sottish, ill-natured rabble', with their 'surly gruffness, bestial stupidity and disgraceful dissoluteness', companies of civic guards were established in most large towns.

Visitors to the United Provinces were ready to contrast the urban to the rural population. William Temple, an Englishman writing in the 1670s, praised the sophistication of the Dutch townsfolk,

1　The merchants and tradesmen, both the greater and the mechanic, living in towns that are of great resort both by strangers and passengers of their own, are more mercurial (wit being sharpened by commerce and conversation of cities), though they are not
5　inventive, which is the gift of warmer heads; yet they are great in imitation, and so far, many times as goes beyond the originals; of mighty industry and constant application to the ends they propose and pursue. They make use of their skills and their wit, to take advantage of other men's folly.

Temple's opinion of the countryfolk was not so high:

10 The Clowns or Boors (as they call them) . . . are a race of people
diligent rather than laborious, dull and slow of understanding, and
not so dealt with by hasty words, but managed easily by fair and
soft, and yielding to plain reason, if you give them time to understand it. In the country and villages not too near the great towns,
15 they seem plain and honest, and content with their own, so that if
in bounty you give them a shilling for what is worth a groat, they
will take the current price, and give you the rest again. If you bid
them take it, they know not what you mean and sometimes ask you
20 if you are a fool. They feed most upon herbs, roots and milks, and
by that means I suppose neither their strength nor vigour seems
answerable to the size or bulk of their bodies.

William Temple clearly makes too sharp a contrast between townsmen
and countryfolk. Firstly, wages on the land were sufficiently high to
attract a large number of seasonal migrants who every summer helped
dig peat and harvest the hay. Secondly, the rural workforce, although
consisting largely of freemen, either cultivating their own plots or
engaged as farm labourers, depended heavily on the urban economy.
Many agricultural workers were employed on the properties of absentee
townsmen; others supplemented their income by manufacturing at home
under contract; all provided for the huge urban market and were reliant
on the network of urban distribution.

The United Provinces was, therefore, a predominantly middle-class
republic. Middle-class patricians dominated town government, the
States-General and most of the provincial estates. The wealth of the
middle class sustained the struggle against Spain. The influence of the
urban middle class also reached deep into the countryside where the rural
workforce became more and more dependent on the towns to buy their
produce. Only in one respect was the triumph of the middle class left
incomplete: in the House of Orange. The *stadholders* preserved the last
relic of the old aristocratic principle and the House of Orange was in the
north all that remained of the great landowning families which had once
held sway in the Netherlands. Around the House clustered a network of
feudal clients drawn from the petty noblemen of the countryside.
Throughout the seventeenth century the issue remained in the balance
whether the government of the United Provinces would remain the
domain of the middle class or whether it would revert to an aristocratic,
semi-monarchial form under the supremacy of the House of Orange.

4 A Golden Age

The seventeenth century was the 'Golden Age' of the United Provinces.

In commerce and trade the Dutch led the way in Europe; their riches and towns impressed all who visited them. The Dutch had in addition stood the test of the war with Spain; later in the century they would success-fully resist both Britain and France. However, it is not just economic and military accomplishments which made the seventeenth century a Dutch Golden Age. In literature, philosophy, science and art, the United Provinces uniquely contributed to the civilisation of contemporary Europe.

In 1609 the catalogue of books in Amsterdam municipal library was found to contain only nine titles in Dutch: all the rest being in Latin or French. Over the following decades this deficiency was remedied and a specifically Dutch literature flourished. In many respects the interest of Dutch writers in composing prose and verse in their native language reflects a growing sense of national identity. The greatest expression of Dutch literary achievement is the States Bible of 1637 (so called because it was commissioned by the States-General), which exercised as pro-found an effect on Dutch writing as the Authorised Version of James I did on English style. Largely because they remain untranslated, though, the literary works of Pieter Hooft (1582–1647), Constantine Huygens (1596–1687) and, preeminently, Joost van den Vondel (1587–1679) are unfamiliar to a European audience. However, in their own country these writers enjoy an acclaim similar to that bestowed in England on Shake-speare and Milton.

Two particular criticisms may, though, be passed on the Dutch literary achievement of the seventeenth century. Firstly, this was a period of linguistic experimentation, itself largely a product of the relative novelty of the Dutch language as a literary vehicle. Much of Dutch prose and verse conveys, therefore, the impression of artificiality and of being forced into a Latin or Italianate strait-jacket. Secondly, most Dutch writers of the Golden Age did not view literature as an end in itself, but as a way of expressing simple moral truths, often of a religious nature. Accordingly, their concern was more for the message than for the medium, even at the expense of style and clarity of expression.

* The United Provinces was above all an 'open society'. It always allowed freedom of conscience and no attempt was ever made to compel persons living there to belong to one special faith. By the 1620s, after the Remonstrant controversy had abated, less concern was shown for pre-venting followers of different religions from worshipping together in public: either as Jews, Anabaptists or Remonstrants. A form of institu-tionalised bribery even permitted Catholic congregations to meet with the full knowledge of local town councils and magistrates. Nor was much concern ever shown for limiting liberty of expression or of the press; largely it was only works of a highly seditious nature which were liable to confiscation. Furthermore, in the big cities little notice was taken of the radical thinker or of intellectual non-conformity. One philosopher who moved to Amsterdam was pleased to write that there 'in the midst of a

great crowd of busy people, more concerned with their own business than curious about that of others . . . I have been able to live as solitary and withdrawn as I would in the most remote of deserts.'

The wide freedom of belief allowed in the United Provinces made it a haven for philosophers. Ironically, therefore, and because the Dutch universities were generally conservative institutions, two of the greatest philosophers working in the United Provinces, Descartes and Spinoza, were of French and of Jewish origin respectively.

The greatest problem which philosophy faced in the early seventeenth century was that the old religious framework of ideas had been torn apart by the Reformation and the Renaissance. It was no longer any good looking to religion for inspiration, for there was no longer any general agreement on what was the right religion to follow. By the end of the sixteenth century, therefore, scepticism was the dominant philosophical mood. Like Montaigne in France, many argued that it was impossible to know anything for certain and that all was in doubt. The furious civil and international wars of the time confirmed the attitude of resignation and of intellectual hopelessness.

The mainstream of philosophy in the United Provinces during the seventeenth century challenged the assumption that it was impossible to know or believe anything. Hugo Grotius (1583–1645) argued that despite the strife of contemporary Europe, laws based on correct reasoning and proper observation could still be found to regulate relations between states. Grotius based his analysis on the following idea:

1 Communities have need of some system of law whereby they may be directly and properly ordered with regard to intercourse and association and although that guidance is in large measure provided by natural reason, it is not provided in sufficient measure and in a
5 direct manner with respect to all matters; therefore it [is] possible for certain special rules of law to be introduced through the practice of these same nations. For just as in one state or province law is introduced by custom, so among the human race as a whole it [is] possible for laws to be introduced by the habitual conduct of
10 nations.

The Jewish philosopher Baruch Spinoza (1632–1677), who lived in Amsterdam, similarly employed a system of reasoning and logical deduction to prove the existence of a single universe governed by general laws. But perhaps the most exciting and important philosophical theses were laid by René Descartes, a French thinker resident in Holland from 1629 to 1648. Descartes began by accepting the outlook of the sceptics and admitting that maybe everything we experienced and saw around us was the creation of a malicious demon who had filled our mind with hallucinations. But from this premise Descartes was able to argue his own existence, the existence of God and, therefore, the reality of our everyday

experiences, including our perception of general principles. In this way
Descartes refuted – at least for the time being – the views of the sceptics.
Let us attempt to follow his reasoning:

1   I resolved to pretend that nothing which had ever entered my mind
    was any more true than the illusions of my dreams. But
    immediately afterwards I became aware that . . . it followed neces-
    sarily that I who thought thus must be something; and observing
5   the truth: *I think therefore I am*, was so certain and so evident that
    all the most extravagant suppositions of the sceptics were not
    capable of shaking it, I judged that I could accept it without scruple
    as the first principle of the philosophy I was seeking . . . Following
    this, reflecting on the fact that I had doubts, and that consequently
10 my being was not perfect, for I saw clearly that it was a greater
    perfection to know than to doubt, I decided to enquire whence I
    had learned to think of something more perfect than myself; and I
    clearly recognised that this must have been from some nature
    which was in fact more perfect . . . which was God . . . This tells us
15 that all our ideas and notions must have some basis in truth, for it
    would not be possible that God, who is all perfect and true, should
    have put them in us unless it were so . . . I should be very pleased to
    continue and to show here the complete chain of other truths that I
    deduced from those first ones but . . . I believe it will be better for
20 me to abstain and mention them only in general terms . . . I have
    for instance observed certain laws which God has so established in
    nature and of which he has impressed such notions in our souls,
    that having reflected on them sufficiently, we cannot doubt that
    they are observed in everything which exists or which happens in
25 the world.

Philosophy spilled over into natural science. In the middle ages
scientists had been content to repeat the outworn ideas of classical
writers, even though they might be clearly at odds with the evidence.
When in doubt medieval scientists took refuge in theological explanations. During the Renaissance the first steps were taken to reexamine
previous interpretations on the basis of experiment and to establish
connections between different observations. The emphasis placed by
Descartes and by the other philosophers on the validity of experience and
on the existence of general laws, encouraged the new trend in scientific
thinking. Partly as a consequence, the United Provinces became one of
Europe's greatest centres for the study of the natural and medical
sciences. It was in Holland that the telescope and microscope were not
only invented but also employed by Christiaan Huygens and Anthonie
van Leeuwenhoek to observe respectively Saturn's rings and protozoa
bacteria. Huygens in addition devised the chronometer, air-pump and

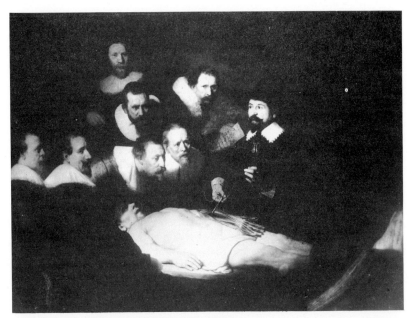

Rembrandt's 'Anatomy Lecture of Dr Tulp'

Rembrandt's 'Night Watch' (The Company of Captain Banning Cocq)

pendulum clock as well as discovering the laws which governed the behaviour of light waves. In Leiden and Amsterdam the Guilds of Surgeons performed every year the dissection of a human corpse, checking their own observations against the accepted textbooks. The *Anatomy Lecture of Dr Tulp*, painted by Rembrandt in 1632, records one such event. By the close of the century Leiden University had become a leading European centre in medical research.

* The achievement of seventeenth-century Dutch civilisation is most closely associated with its artists: most notably Vermeer, Steen, Hals, De Hooch and, of course, Rembrandt. The distinctive feature of the Dutch school of art is the simplicity of its subject matter and its realistic portrayal of everyday events. The technical accomplishment of the Dutch artists was built on a tradition which stretched back in the Netherlands to the Flemish school of the late middle ages. The choice of subject matter and the relatively small size of Dutch paintings had, though, a quite different origin: market demand.

The Dutch middle class, and many of their social inferiors, were avid collectors of paintings. One English traveller reported in 1640 that, 'All in general strive to adorn their houses, especially the outer or street rooms, with costly pieces; butchers and bakers, yea many times black-smiths, cobblers etcetera will have some pictures or other by their forge or in their stall. Such is the general notion, inclination and delight that these people have to paintings.' In other countries where the patrons of artists were the great nobility, the subject matter of the pictures they commi-ssioned reflected aristocratic values: martial scenes, legends from anti-quity and larger-than-life figures in court dress. The paintings needed to be vast so as to fill the walls of stately homes and impress visitors. By contrast, in the United Provinces, where the middle class provided the main market for the artist's trade, the pictures had to be smaller (to fit into narrow homes) and had also to conform to a humbler set of values. Depictions of splendour and extravagance had little meaning for the citizens of Amsterdam or Haarlem. Objects which were instead familiar to a more commonplace way of life were thus demanded of native artists and they, who had to make a living, complied.

The typical subject matter of Dutch paintings consisted of scenes from everyday life: townscapes, seascapes and landscapes; happy events at mealtime or while out skating; views showing tidy homes and well-scrubbed tiles; still lifes of familiar objects. Portraits, though, were the most common genre and many were group portraits. Leading guilds-men, directors of charities and units of officers of the civic guard fre-quently had their portraits painted to record for posterity their common achievement as citizens. Arguably the greatest painting of the Dutch seventeenth century, Rembrandt's *Night Watch*, commemorated a com-pany of the civic guard in Amsterdam.

The Dutch art of the seventeenth century, like the Republic itself, was profoundly middle class. However, the exception we noted in the last

'A Woman and her Maid in a Courtyard' by Pieter de Hooch

section persisted even in art. Around the House of Orange gathered a 'court culture' which was very different from the predominant cultural forms of Dutch society. The *stadholder* Frederick Henry was thus the patron of Van Dyck and Rubens, who were the foremost court artists of western Europe. Dianas, nymphs and resplendent Italianate landscapes were the stock of Dutch 'court art'. Even in architecture, the House of Orange patronised neo-classical forms which had more in keeping with the stylistic grandeur of the great houses in the Spanish provinces than the humble baroque of contemporary Holland. In their extravagance and courtly magnificence the *stadholders* behaved more like great aristocrats than the 'first servants' of a middle-class republic.

5 William II

In the preceding two sections of this chapter we have indicated the peculiar position held by the House of Orange in the United Provinces. This middle-class republic had as its leading and most powerful family a dynasty of aristocrats. The essential difference of the House of Orange found expression in art and architecture and a 'courtly style'. In addition, around the House gathered a network of dependents consisting mainly of remnants of the nobility, while the private wealth of the Orange family derived overwhelmingly from its landed estates and not from trade.

It would be wrong, however, to conceive of the position held by the House of Orange only in class terms: as aristocracy amongst middle class. The House of Orange enjoyed a reputation and influence which transcended class boundaries. William (I) of Orange had led the revolt against Spanish rule; his sons had continued the struggle and brought it to a successful conclusion. In the Remonstrant crisis the *stadholder* had intervened to resolve an internal problem which threatened civil war. Furthermore, by Maurice's actions in 1618–19 the House had demonstrated its political and religious sympathies. It had stood up for the preservation of Calvinist orthodoxy and for unity against the dominance of Holland. For this reason, the House of Orange could normally count on the support of the clergy and of the six provinces – and on the opposition of Holland.

It is convenient to see the House of Orange as the 'unofficial monarchy' of the United Provinces. To an extent, this was how the House was viewed at the time – as entrusted by divine right to be the guiding light of the Republic. In the words of the Dutch poet, Vondel, the *stadholders* were 'those who by God as helmsmen are ordained, to serve the common weal.' For their part, the *stadholder* Frederick Henry and his son and successor, William II, happily assumed a semi-royal role within the government and politics of the Republic. Both pursued a dynastic policy and established a close link by marriage with the House of Stuart. William II married Mary Stuart, Charles I of England's daughter, and the possibility of a marriage between the Prince of Wales (subsequently Charles II) and an Orange princess existed for a time. During the 1640s Frederick Henry tried to have the United Provinces intervene in the English Civil War on the royalist side. At the same time, Frederick Henry, using the excuse of the war with Spain, made some preliminary reforms in the government of the United Provinces and established a cabinet (the *Secreet Besogne*) which reduced the power of the States-General. In the dynastic and centralising policies of the House of Orange the historian Pieter Geyl has seen a 'monarchical principle' at work.

    ⋆ Once peace was made with Spain in 1648, a reaction set in against the influence and ambition of the House of Orange. The lead was taken by the estates of Holland and partly for this reason the estates of the other provinces rallied round William II, who had taken over after the death of his father in 1647 as *stadholder* of six of the seven provinces. The issue over which conflict broke out was Holland's refusal to maintain the large army which had been gathered in the recently ended war. William II opposed the disbandment of the Dutch forces. Firstly, he hoped to use them against England and, secondly, he knew the power which command of the army gave him in political affairs.

In 1649 the Holland estates ordered army units in their provinces to dissolve. The States-General, at William's bidding, declared this order illegal, but Holland persisted in disbanding the army. In July 1650 William with the consent of the States-General organised a coup in Holland reminiscent of that performed by his uncle Maurice in 1618. William invaded Holland and purged the local town councils on account of their alleged 'breaking and dissolving the Union'. On 30 July he entered The Hague and put the Holland estates under arrest.

Had William lived longer, then perhaps the whole constitution of the United Provinces might have been revised to allow firmer central direction under the supremacy of the House of Orange. But by the end of the year William was dead of smallpox. His son, the future William III, was conceived but not yet born. For the time being, therefore, there was no successor who could take over the commanding position which William had seized.

* In the confusion which followed William II's death, the Holland estates were able to re-establish their position. A Grand Assembly was called by Holland in 1651. Made up of large delegations from all the provinces, the Grand Assembly had the right to make laws without reference either to the local estates or to the States-General. The Assembly was manoeuvred into agreeing with Holland that for the time being a *stadholder* was unnecessary and that all the powers which had been vested in this office should revert to the provincial estates.

Of course, in the aftermath of the Grand Assembly the estates of Holland once more took the lead in the making of domestic and foreign policy. Under the guidance of Holland's Grand Pensionary, Johan De Witt, the United Provinces engaged in wars against Sweden (1658–60) and England (1652–54; 1665–67), mainly in order to preserve Dutch commercial supremacy against the challenge of new economic rivals. De Witt's successful handling of these wars transformed him into a statesman of the first rank. To restrain Louis XIV of France's expansionist ambitions, De Witt established the Triple Alliance of 1668 with his former adversaries, England and Sweden, and made the United Provinces the founding member of an international coalition.

De Witt's reputation hung on his conduct of foreign affairs. When his foreign policy faltered, he himself fell. In 1670 Charles II of England forsook his alliance with the Dutch and came to terms with France in the

Treaty of Dover. Two years later, the new partners declared war on the United Provinces. Although the Dutch fleet proved sufficient to defend the coastline of Holland and Zealand against the English navy, the land war with France resulted in the immediate invasion of large parts of the Republic. De Witt paid dearly for this major setback. Already the son of William II, William III, had shown himself an able administrator and commander. De Witt had endeavoured to use William's talents while still preventing him from assuming the offices and ambitions of his father. But now, with only flooded polders protecting Holland from the army of Louis XIV, the estates of Holland demanded De Witt's resignation and proclaimed William *stadholder*. De Witt accordingly gave up the office of Grand Pensionary. But this was insufficient as far as the frightened populace of The Hague were concerned. He was caught by the mob, was lynched and his body was hacked to pieces for grisly souvenirs.

Under William III's leadership (1672–1702), the United Provinces recovered the lands seized by Louis XIV. Hereafter, the Dutch were partners in a series of fresh coalitions against France. It is testimony to the central role played by the United Provinces in the international diplomacy of the period that the three great peace conferences of Louis XIV's reign were held on Dutch soil – at Nijmwegen in 1678, Ruyswick in 1697 and (although held after William III's death) at Utrecht in 1714. But despite William's achievements on the international stage and his appointment as King of England in 1689, the United Provinces continued to waver between a monarchical form of government under the House of Orange, and a narrowly republican one under the guidance of Holland. On William III's death in 1702, a second 'stadholderless' period began under a Grand Pensionary of Holland which endured until 1747. A French invasion in that year provoked the same reaction as in 1672: an Orangist revolution during which William IV was appointed *stadholder*. Hereafter, the threat of revolution from below bound the restored House of Orange to the ruling class of Holland, and the government of the Republic limped along in timid compromise until the abolition of the United Provinces by the French in 1795.

Making Notes on 'The United Provinces 1609–1650'

The following heading and questions will help you make suitable notes:

1.   Remonstrants and Contra-Remonstrants
1.1. Government
1.2. Holland and Oldenbarnevelt
1.3. Erastianism and Arminianism
1.4. Religious conflict

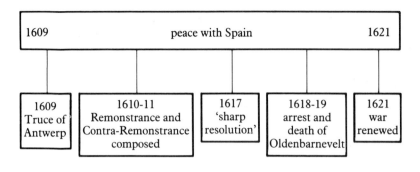

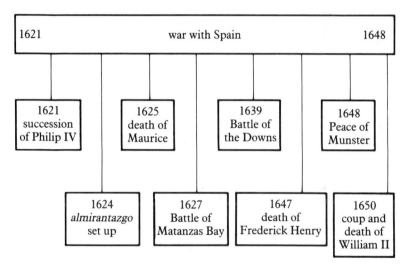

Summary – The United Provinces, 1609–48

1.5. The victory of the Contra-Remonstrants
Would you agree with the view that the Remonstrant crisis was caused
less by religion than by arguments over the way the United Provinces
ought to be governed?
2.   The war with Spain
2.1. Renewal of the war
2.2. Stalemate
2.3. The economic war
2.4. The Peace of Münster

List the reasons for the Spanish failure to subdue the Dutch in the period 1621–48
3.   Economy and society
3.1. Trade
3.2. Finance, industry and agriculture
3.3. Social classes
In what ways was the United Provinces 'a predominantly middle-class republic?'
4.   A golden age
4.1. Literature
4.2. Philosophy and science
4.3. Art
In what ways did Dutch art mirror Dutch society in the first half of the seventeenth century?
5.   William II
5.1. The House of Orange
5.2. The crisis of 1650
5.3. The United Provinces 1650–1795
To what extent did the crisis of 1650 reveal that the problems which had earlier caused the Remonstrant crisis had not yet been resolved?

Answering source-based questions on 'The United Provinces, 1609–1650'

1 The Remonstrant crisis

Read the English ambassador's account of the government of the United Provinces on page 79 and the report of the conversation with Oldenbarnevelt on page 82. Answer the following questions:

a)   Later on in his account the writer of the first passage refers to the United Provinces as the 'Disunited Provinces'. In what ways might the political organisation of the United Provinces, as described here, make for disunity?

b)   What other elements of disunity in the United Provinces are identified by Oldenbarnevelt in the second passage?

c)   What remedy does Oldenbarnevelt suggest for healing these divisions?

d)   To what extent, if at all, would Oldenbarnevelt's remedy have compromised his own beliefs?

e)   Explain what you understand by the terms 'theocracy' and 'erastianism'. Using the evidence of the reported conversation, explain why Oldenbarnevelt would have been more likely to subscribe to the second principle.

2 Dutch Society

Read the two extracts on Dutch urban and rural society, which are given on pages 92–93. Answer the following questions:

a)   What does the author believe to be the particular qualities of the Dutch townsfolk? How convincing do you find his explanations for their special skills?

b)   Explain what the author might have meant when he wrote that the countryfolk were 'diligent rather than laborious'.

c)   What does the diet of the rural population suggest about the type of agriculture practised in the United Provinces?

d)   What light do these extracts throw on the strengths and weaknesses of the Dutch economy in the seventeenth century?

3 The Golden Age

Read the extract written by Grotius on page 95 and passage taken from Descartes' *Discourse on Method* on page 96. Look at the two pictures by Rembrandt on page 97 and the picture by De Hooch on page 99.
Answer the following questions:

a)   Who were 'the sceptics' mentioned on line 6 of the passage written by Descartes?

b)   How do Grotius and Descartes arrive at their respective conclusions? What methods of deduction do they share?

c)   What does the science being practised in Rembrandt's *Anatomy Lecture* owe to the type of philosophical method practised by Grotius and Descartes?

d)   Although the techniques and subject-matter of Rembrandt's *Night Watch* and of De Hooch's *Backyard Scene* differ greatly, in what way were they both nevertheless aimed at the same sort of audience? Explain your answer fully.

CHAPTER 7

Analysis: the Rise of the United Provinces

1 War, Government and the Economy

Any explanation for the rise of the United Provinces must concern itself with the economic achievements on which Dutch greatness rested. The foundation built in the late sixteenth century was extended during the next century. The trade and industry of the United Provinces continued to prosper while that of the south only slowly recovered to early six-teenth-century levels. Above all else, it was the arrival of capital and of merchants and craftsmen fleeing from persecution or the depression in the southern Netherlands which provided the reservoir of technical skills and riches on which the Republic built its fortunes. The growth of the cloth industry in Leiden during the first decades of the seventeenth century depended, for instance, on craftsmen who had moved to the town from the old textile-producing centre of Hondschoote in Flanders. The tax registers of Amsterdam show that a third of the town's richest citizens were refugees from the south. In addition, the blockade of Antwerp, 'legalised' by the 1648 Peace of Münster, had the effect of further diverting trade away from the southern provinces towards the north – in particular to the port of Amsterdam.

Financial conditions in the United Provinces ensured that the money accumulated there was employed productively. Already in the sixteenth century the shortage of agricultural land to be bought had had the effect of pushing investment into trade and industry. The development in the seventeenth century of banking and joint-stock enterprises harnessed additional reserves of wealth for business ventures. It may well be, as some economic historians have argued, that the United Provinces was the first European country to achieve a stable pattern of growth, but this theory cannot be tested. Certainly, though, by 1650 the Republic pro-vided the bulk of European shipping, the principal European com-modity market and centre for marine insurance. It was also the largest provider of cured fish and the second greatest (after England) producer of cloth. The innovations which made possible the 'agricultural revolu-tion' of the eighteenth century also had their origins in the United Provinces where new methods of farming were pioneered.

* The economy sustained the long war with Spain and supported the rising burden of military expenditure. Without its formidable resources the two million Dutch could not otherwise have defended their country against a Spanish empire which, albeit in decline, still numbered in the Iberian peninsula alone some ten million persons. By 1640 the Republic was spending 19 million florins a year on its armed services: a fivefold increase over what had been paid out in the early 1590s. Taxation and

state borrowing drew private wealth into public coffers. By 1651 Holland's debt stood at 153 million florins which was the equivalent of 12 whole treasure fleets. The high level of military expenditure was largely due to the cost of fortifications. By the middle of the seventeenth century almost every Dutch town was encircled by massive ramparts and it is this feature of military geography which, as we have seen, partly explains the static quality of the land-war with Spain between 1621 and 1648.

War aided the Dutch economy only in the phase before 1609. It was in this earlier period that there occurred the massive disruption to the southern economy and the 'Great Migration' to the north, both of which benefited the United Provinces. After 1621, though, only the munitions industry prospered. Rising military expenditure diverted resources into unproductive channels which yielded little by way of increased demand for products or services. The army skimmed off labour which could have been better employed in industry or agriculture. The indirect advantage of the war, in allowing Dutch traders the excuse to invade Spanish markets in the Indies, was outweighed by the damage inflicted on shipping and fishing in the blockade of the 1620s and 1630s. No other testimony is needed as to the harm which war did to the economy than the pressure applied in the 1640s by the towns of Holland for an end to hostilities. By this time even Amsterdam, the dominant voice in the war party of the 1620s, had realised the benefits of peace.

* The greatest service brought by war to the United Provinces was in reducing the tensions caused by the untidy government of the country. In wartime all the provinces had to recognise Holland's leadership, for it was Holland's wealth which sustained the military budget. Similarly, the ruling classes in the towns and the estates of Holland had to put up with the influence of the House of Orange which provided both military leadership and the dynasty of *stadholders* which seemed to embody the sense of national purpose. Once peace was made, the conflicts implicit in the decentralised government of the United Provinces erupted – as in 1618 and 1650 even to the extent of threatening a civil war. As one Dutch pamphleteer, addressing his homeland in 1650, remarked, 'War was for you a bond of union and unity. Peace brings quarrels and disunity.'

By the same token, though, the war with Spain hindered the further development of political institutions. There was little opportunity while the conflict was going on for reforming the clumsy structure of government; by the time peace was made the framework was too well established for a radical and lasting revision: as the fate of the first 'stadholderless' period makes clear. Until the middle of the eighteenth century the United Provinces experienced, therefore, just variations on older themes as the constitutional battle between Holland, the other six provinces and the House of Orange took its course.

2 Broader Explanations

If we ignore the fine brushwork of historical events and concentrate on the wider strokes, an alternative explanation for the rise of the United Provinces may be perceived. The early modern period represents a time of economic transformation. The old feudal order was being eased out and being replaced by one based on capitalist principles. The transition was, of course, a gradual one; it proceeded not so much country by country as by area and region. Yet by the end of the eighteenth century western Europe stood demonstrably on the edge of the industrial revolution; three centuries before, its base was almost totally agricultural. The United Provinces led the way in this change. It was a middle-class society thriving on industry and commerce before any other. Thus the Dutch could make the most of the development of capitalism and of the opening of new markets.

Modern liberal writers on politics are fond of pointing out that a middle-class state based on the principles of private profit will be broadly tolerant and respectful of personal liberty. This perception is contentious, but not original – for in his description of the United Provinces written in the 1670s William Temple made the same observation. Undoubtedly though, and whatever the cause, at a time when most European states operated a machinery of terror, often in the name of religion, the United Provinces was remarkably free. The urban élites made little effort to establish conformity even in religious practices. As a consequence philosophy and science could flourish there. Also, because the Republic was dominated by an urban middle class, it developed a style of painting of remarkable distinction. Whereas most other European countries were overawed by an aristocratic and court culture, the civilisation of the United Provinces was one of sober virtues and well-scrubbed floors.

* The Dutch economic and cultural achievement did not endure. By the eighteenth century even its painting had become stylised and capable of only technical accomplishments. The leading philosophers and scientists of the day set up in England and Germany, and (except in medicine) the United Provinces became relegated to the status of an intellectual backwater. Although the Dutch economy probably did not go entirely into decline, it clearly ceased to grow. England and France outstripped the Dutch in commerce and trade, and their protectionist measures deprived the Dutch of the overseas markets upon which they depended. James Boswell, visiting Holland in the 1760s, found its once great towns 'sadly decayed' and crowds of unemployed on the streets. In Leiden the manufacturing of cloth contracted during the eighteenth century by almost two-thirds. The proportion of Dutch shipping in the Baltic trade fell by a half. Due to the encroachments of other countries' fishing fleets, the herring industry collapsed. In addition, the continued high level of taxation drove enterprising Dutch abroad, where they could

ply their skill and ingenuity for better reward.

The Dutch Golden Age lasted therefore barely a century. It is this brief period of flowering which prompted one historian's remark that perhaps, after all, the Golden Age was a purely accidental event and that we should seek the causes of Dutch greatness in the weakness of the Republic's neighbours. Certainly, for much of the seventeenth century the states of Europe were racked by civil war. France, England and the German lands were sufficiently divided within themselves to be unable to counter the rising economic power of the Dutch. Once their fortunes were restored strong measures could be introduced to deprive the Dutch of the foreign trade on which their prosperity depended and competing industrial organisations could be set up. War did the rest. While in the second half of the seventeenth century the Dutch might still hold their own against England and France, their participation in the War of the Spanish Succession (1702–1713) left the country financially and militarily exhausted. The proof was here that the Dutch did not have the resources to play a major role in European affairs and that the next century could indeed belong to England, France and Prussia.

Making Notes on *'Analysis: the Rise of the United Provinces'*

This chapter is primarily designed to draw together themes which have been dealt with separately in Chapter 6. The analysis should provide additionally a springboard for ideas and interpretations which will help you frame arguments of your own when tackling essay questions.

1.   War, government and the economy
1.1. Reasons for Dutch prosperity
1.2. War and the economy
1.3. War and government
2.   Broader explanations
2.1. Capitalism and the Golden Age
2.2. Decline

Answering essay questions on *'The United Provinces 1609–1650'*

In A-level examinations, questions on the United Provinces in the seventeenth century are not such 'certainties' as questions on the Revolt. Nevertheless, they have sufficient frequency to make this topic worth studying for examination purposes. Questions are on the whole evenly split between political and economic issues:

'Why were the Dutch so prosperous in the seventeenth century?'

'Explain the growth of Dutch commerce in the early seventeenth century.'

' "Overseas trading bases were the cause of Dutch prosperity in the seventeenth century." Do you agree?'

The material for all these essays is included in the section on 'Economy and Society' in the preceding chapter and is summarised with some added detail and interpretation in the Analysis. You may plan the first two essays with a 'because' scheme: do you realise that 'Explain the growth of *x*' means the same as 'Why did *x* grow?! Decide on a number (at least three and no more than five) of direct answers to the question, each beginning with the word 'because'. Place them in order of importance. This will provide you with a paragraph plan for your answer. Will you start with the most important or the least important point?

You should question the assumption in the third question, for as you will now have read, overseas bases were not 'the cause of Dutch prosperity'. However, you must show some appreciation of the terms of the question – do not dismiss the quotation out of hand. Begin by outlining the economic role played by Dutch factories abroad, then move on to better explanations for Dutch prosperity.

On political matters, questions tend to be broad. So you are unlikely to be asked specifically the motives of Oldenbarnevelt or William II. Nor will you be expected to display any detailed knowledge of the Remonstrant crisis.

'How did the House of Orange contribute to the development of the Netherlands in the seventeenth century?'

'In what respects were the United Provinces of the seventeenth century more obviously 'Disunited Provinces'?'

These are very loosely phrased questions and thus there is no one obvious or right way of answering them. In assessing the role of the House of Orange in the politics of the United Provinces you will need to consider separately the House's 'unifying function', its position of *de facto* monarchy and the conflict with the estates of Holland (both in 1618 and in 1650). In the second question you should give a detailed description of the government of the United Provinces relating this to the issues which fostered disunity. But also analyse the factors and influences which prevented the Republic from splitting up altogether: the House of Orange; the war with Spain; a tradition of tolerance; the dependence of the six provinces on Holland.

Very occasionally questions, or parts of questions, occur on the Golden Age and on Dutch cultural achievements:

'Do you agree that in terms of economic and cultural achievement the United Provinces was the most advanced state in seventeenth-century Europe?'

Tempting though it may be, do not simply write a description of the Dutch economy and culture of the seventeenth century. The question has a catch: 'most advanced'. Your essay, therefore, will need to begin with a paragraph on how economic and cultural achievement may be measured. Also you will need to bring into your essay references to other countries. So you will have to consider briefly the economic and cultural achievement of, say, contemporary England, France or Spain and judge whether these states reached a higher level of achievement than the United Provinces.

Sources on 'The Netherlands: Revolt and Independence, 1550–1650'

The principal source collections are

1. **E. H. Kossman** and **A. F. Mellinck** *Texts concerning the Revolt of the Netherlands* (Cambridge University Press, 1974) and
2. **Herbert Rowen** *The Low Countries in Early Modern Times* (Macmillan, 1972)

The following, which was originally published in 1673, has been edited by Sir George Clark

3. **William Temple** *Observations Upon the United Provinces of the Netherlands* (Oxford University Press, 2nd edition, 1972)

Accounts of the Netherlands in the early seventeenth century are most notably preserved in

4. **C. H. Firth** *Stuart Tracts* (Constable, 1903)

Acknowledgements

Acknowledgement is given for use of extracts as follows:
M. C. Rady, *Emperor Charles V* (Longman) page 10
Joy Shakespeare and **Maria Dowling**, 'Religion and politics in Mid-Tudor England', *Bulletin of the Institute of Historical Research* pages 10–11
James Bruce Ross and **Mary Martin McLaughlin**, *The Portable Renaissance Reader* (Penguin/Viking) page 12
Herbert H. Rowen, *The Low Countries in Early Modern Times* (Macmillan) pages 21–3, 42, 44, 49–59
Peter Pierson, *Philip II of Spain* (Thames and Hudson) pages 23–4
E. H. Kossmann and **A. F. Mellinck**, *Texts Concerning the Revolt of the Netherlands* (Cambridge University Press) pages 30–1, 50–1
C. H. Firth, *Stuart Tracts* (Archibald Constable & Co) page 61
ed. **Sir George Clark**, *Sir William Temple's Observations Upon the United Provinces of the Netherlands* (Oxford University Press) page 79, 92–3
British Library Department of MSS, Harley MS 4298, page 82
Public Record Office, London, page 86 (I owe this reference to the kindness of Mr Andrew Thrush)
Charles S. Edwards, *Hugo Grotius: The Miracle of Holland* (Nelson-Hall Chicago) page 95
trans. **F. E. Sutcliffe**, *Descartes' Discourse on Method and other Writings* (Penguin) page 96

developments in Dutch art, science and philisophy during this period

Your school or local library may have on its shelves a dusty copy of

J. L. Motley *Rise of the Dutch Republic* (1856 and many later editions)

Motley is long, but never dull. He has an eye for the telling anecdote and has a vivid prose style. His narrative can still, more than 130 years later, be gripping.

The works of Professors W. S. Maltby and J. W. Smit, both of whom are cited by name in the main text are

W. S. Maltby *Alba: A Biography of Fernando Alvarez de Toledo 1507–1582* (University of California Press, 1983)

J. W. Smit 'The Present Position of Studies Regarding the Revolt of the Netherlands', *Britain and the Netherlands*, I, edited by J. S. Bromley and E. H. Kossman (Chatto and Windus, 1960)

Further Reading

The standard works on the Dutch Revolt and on the United Provinces used to be

Pieter Geyl *The Revolt of the Netherlands* (Williams and Norgate, 1932), and *The Netherlands in the Seventeenth Century* 2 vols (Benn, 1961–64)

Both have now been superseded, although they can still be found on the shelves of most school libraries. The most up-to-date and easily available books on the Netherlands are

Geoffrey Parker *The Dutch Revolt* 2nd edition (Penguin, 1985)
Jonathan Israel *The Dutch Republic and the Hispanic World 1606–1661* (Oxford University Press, 1982)
Charles Wilson *The Dutch Republic* (World University Library, 1968)

All these are worth consulting if you want additional information, but the first two give a very detailed treatment of events which can leave the reader confused.
Two recent publications designed primarily for students are

K. W. Swart *William the Silent and the Revolt of the Netherlands* (Historical Association Pamphlet, 1978)
History Today vol 34, July–August 1984 (a series of short articles commemorating William of Orange)

Individual items in

Geoffrey Parker *Spain and the Netherlands 1559–1659* (Fontana, 1979)

should be within the range of the upper-sixth former. The book contains a collection of the author's essays on the Dutch Revolt and Republic.
It is with caution that one recommends to an A-level student a full-length book. But four do stand out as eminently readable and fascinating in their content:

C. V. Wedgwood *William the Silent* (Jonathan Cape, 1944) – an elegantly written biography which conveys the atmosphere of the times
C. R. Boxer *The Dutch Seaborne Empire 1600–1800* (Hutchinson, 1965) – on Dutch trade, expansion and society overseas
Geoffrey Parker *The Army of Flanders and the Spanish Road* (Cambridge University Press, 1972) – how the Spanish army in the Netherlands lived, fought and mutinied
J. L. Price *Culture and Society in the Dutch Republic during the Seventeenth Century* (Batsford, 1974) – explains in simple terms the main

116   Acknowledgements

The author and publishers would like to thank the following for their permission to use copyright illustrations:
Musées Royaux des Beaux-Arts de Belgique: Cover; Staatliche Kunstsammlungen, Kassel: p. 18; Mary Evans Picture Library: p 22; Kunsthistorisches Museum, Wien: p 25; The Mansell Collection Ltd: p 97 top and bottom; Courtesy of the Trustees of the National Gallery, London: p 99; Collins Publishers for a graph from Geoffrey Parker, *Spain and the Netherlands 1559–1659*: p 63.

Index